T0383183

Engineering Solutions to America's Healthcare Challenges

Engineering Solutions to America's Healthcare Challenges

Ryan Burge

CRC Press
Taylor & Francis Group
Boca Raton   London   New York

CRC Press is an imprint of the
Taylor & Francis Group, an **informa** business

A PRODUCTIVITY PRESS BOOK

CRC Press
Taylor & Francis Group
6000 Broken Sound Parkway NW, Suite 300
Boca Raton, FL 33487-2742

Printed on acid-free paper
Version Date: 20131017

International Standard Book Number-13: 978-1-4665-8355-9 (Hardback)

Visit the Taylor & Francis Web site at
http://www.taylorandfrancis.com

and the CRC Press Web site at
http://www.crcpress.com

This book is dedicated to healthcare professionals everywhere. Theirs is the noblest of all callings.

Contents

Acknowledgments

I love to make things better. As the environment becomes increasingly complex, I feel that process improvement and quality are critical to an organization's sustainability in its marketplace. I enjoy my work because I can actually see real change in the way organizations function, and how these changes positively impact consumers and members of society. My passion is inspired and supported by many others, including my wife, Maghan, and our parents for their unwavering support; my sisters and their families; and all experts and professionals who spent time providing information critical to the purpose of this book. To my amazing editor and friend, Candi Cross: Thank you for your devotion to this book and the long hours turning it into a work that may open eyes to the world of healthcare quality. And lastly, to Kris Mednansky, senior editor at CRC Press: I owe you big time for your flexibility, understanding, and unwavering support during the completion of this book.

About the Author

Ryan Burge is a leading consultant for the private sector and government with experience as an industrial engineer, certified Lean Six Sigma Master Black Belt, and change agent. Recognized nationwide as an innovative consultant focused on operational improvement, financial and risk analysis, and corporate strategy, Burge has garnered meaningful results for the federal government, the military services, global and Fortune 500 companies, and most recently, Booz Allen Hamilton.

Burge has held board memberships with the American Society for Quality (ASQ) Maryland/DC section and the Maryland Performance Excellence Foundation (MPEF)—a Malcolm Baldrige program for the state of Maryland. He has collaborated with industry executives on a biomedical and biotechnology special interest group for ASQ which engages the regulatory, industry, and academic communities with honest, informed, advanced discussion of biomedical and biotechnical research and topics as related to quality principles and practices.

A proponent of positive public awareness and supporting programs that foster the next generation of business leaders, Burge is an author of articles and books on quality improvement, health systems, and executive leadership. He is also a member of the following organizations: American Society for Quality, Institute of Industrial Engineers (IIE), and the National Association for Healthcare Quality (NAHQ).

Burge holds a BS in industrial engineering from the University of Oklahoma, an MS in engineering management from the George Washington University, and a joint MBA/MA in government from the Johns Hopkins University. He currently resides in Alexandria, Virginia, and can be reached via his consulting firm at http://www.boulevardcg.com or by email at ryan.burge@boulevardcg.com.

Introduction

In April 2009, the World Health Organization (WHO) declared a level 4 category alert to the threat of swine flu becoming a pandemic. More than 90 cases were reported in the United States within four days. More than 120 deaths occurred in Mexico. Cases popped up in Germany, New Zealand, Spain, and several other countries. Sick travelers were screened with thermal imaging devices that detect fever. That was just the beginning of the nefarious swine flu pandemic.

Armed with knowledge and an appointment for a Tamiflu shot, you and I may have felt safe. But what if we still contracted the virus? What if it happened again today? What would the treatment process be? Morale of the facility we're admitted to? Condition of the tools that touch our skin? Level of education and concern of the individuals who care for us? Quality of technology that supports our treatment plan?

Years ago, these probing questions would have been dismissed as paranoia. Today, as deep and complex debates pointing to our care rage on, these are genuine concerns that are justified due to widespread fear, confusion, and distrust of healthcare.

What good are genomics, imaging equipment, digital medical records, ancient healing practices, or the next line of expensive vitamins when more than 50 million people cannot afford an asthma inhaler, glucose-monitoring kit, dental cleaning, or comfortable mattress to sleep on? Is the culprit people, the government, processes, systems, cost, complacency, poverty, or the steel-reinforced greed that has barred basic compassion from entering discussion on healthcare and, ultimately, policy?

This book dips into each area as an enabler, extracting information that has been hidden far too long in the hazardous waste container, unseen and unchecked. But it does not aim to offer even more depressing news without resolution. This book is *not* a medical guide, policy declaration, antigovernment manifesto, legal dictionary, infomercial for technology or medical tourism, socialist rant, or long-winded letter to United States President Barack Obama.

Engineering Solutions to America's Healthcare Challenges introduces phenomenal people—true saviors of humankind and pioneers of medicine—as well as technologies, systems, and processes that are unfolding in hospitals, clinics, community centers, universities, and the White House to repair and refresh healthcare in the United States. The author, a process improvement consultant, believes that no matter how much "official" healthcare reform comes from the U.S. administration, decision makers, doctors, nurses, insurance providers, and patients must create and experience the entire picture as one system.

The book offers solutions that present a systems approach to changing the way millions of healthcare employees do business and the way that consumers take care of their own bodies.

How do we sum up an industry? In our discussion, the components of healthcare run concurrent with the definition by the American Hospital Association's Health Research and Educational Trust: preventive, diagnostic, therapeutic, rehabilitative, maintenance, mental health, or palliative care, and sale or dispensing of a drug, device, piece of equipment, or other item in accordance with a prescription. In the economic landscape alone, Economy Watch (http://www.economywatch.com) reports that the United States healthcare industry constitutes 15 percent of the economy of the country. And finally, the Bureau of Labor Statistics confirms that employment in healthcare has continued to grow even during the recent three-year recession span, adding 559,000 jobs since the beginning of the recession in December 2007.

Chapter 1 focuses on the importance of being proactive about your own state of health. To not address the topic of self-care while talking about high-level processes, technology, and officials that dictate how our healthcare system will operate is like talking about what car to buy without considering its performance type, engine, fuel capacity, or motor. In getting to the root of a system, you must examine every part of the sum—in this case, living and breathing people. The life cycle of improvement begins with the individual person, spans all healthcare workers and facilities involved in the care of that person, and ends with the government, which oversees our nation's healthcare system. Chapter 1 provides context for the more technical aspects of the book to come.

Industrial engineering is comprised of case studies in which to benchmark for process improvement. Benchmarking does involve emulating the habits and examples set by other companies to improve your own, and it requires ongoing attention. This practice begins here.

Places like Progressive Medical Centers of America eliminate waste in spending, time, and labor while somehow giving the patient more control than he or she may have had over his or her own body before visiting a physician. *People* like Dr. Robert Zarr, a well-known pediatrician based in Washington, DC, focus on quality improvement initiatives on topics about which we don't often hear from the medical world: asthma management, injury prevention, and literacy, among others. And *organizations* like the Society for Health Systems provide the supportive backbone needed to enhance the career development and continuing education of professionals worldwide who use industrial and management engineering expertise for productivity and quality improvement in the healthcare industry.

Chapter 2 introduces how industrial engineering practices are shaping healthcare. The chapter aims to demonstrate that systems thinking should be the foundation for every aspect of healthcare because of its innate comprehensive problem-solving methodology. Starting with analysis of the Institute of Medicine's six aims for healthcare to satisfy—safety, effectiveness, efficiency, timeliness, family-centered focus, and equity—the chapter introduces applications and examples of the theory of constraints, Six Sigma, design of experiments, and other signature methods that can apply to healthcare.

Chapter 3 discusses care ethics, which seeks to include all people—regardless of age, ethnicity, sexual orientation, or insurance status—in the practice of medicine and the policies that govern those actions. Care ethics also seeks to include mental health in the overarching field of healthcare and how that field is improved upon and managed. Beginning with the story of Esmin Green, who died on the floor of an emergency room after waiting hours for medical attention, the chapter focuses on quality of care that is broken due to a lack of accountability in hospital administration.

Other examples, such as the Texas Department of State Health Services, show the consequences of ignoring quality aims. Process improvement experts weigh in on the case for choice and more specialized facilities under a holistic system of healthcare.

It's no wonder that President Obama included $19 billion in computerized medical record funding in the $787 billion American Recovery and Reinvestment Act of 2009. Technology and "green" are now joined at the hip. Perhaps there is no greater industry than healthcare in which the pair is being vigorously tested and applied on a daily basis. Green technology is changing the face of healthcare in every way imaginable, and Chapter 4 discusses some of the applications as they relate to efficiency and elimination of wastes of time, money, and human resources.

Still a new concept in some circles, medical tourism has both a mystique to it and a true authority over healthcare that is not fully realized in the United States. Chapter 5 discusses the growing trends and implications of medical tourism, drawing a map from Cuba to India. The book can't avoid describing this "medical trade," given the amount of people and other resources involved.

From a systems-oriented perspective, medical tourism offers choice, cost reduction, and innovation. Its promises may seem foreign to those who haven't been put in the predicament of seriously having to consider traveling thousands of miles away for a procedure. However, from the position of Dr. Agolli and others who wouldn't hesitate to send their patients on a plane for treatment, the quest to solve medical problems and heal their patients outweighs fear of the unknown. The chapter largely points out that we have access to a global health network, not just means within our own country.

Is insurance a safety net or is it an illusion? Insurance has been a highly contested component of healthcare for decades. Chapter 6 addresses the roles of insurance and perspectives that have manifested into actual plans and rules to live or die by. Experts answer tough questions and provide understanding about such options as universal healthcare, consumer-driven insurance, talking points from the Physicians for a National Health Program, the Obama administration's provisions, Medicaid, and Medicare.

A longtime consultant describes how industrial engineers are helping healthcare facilities everywhere examine their admission, authorization, documentation, and case management processes to support financial reimbursement of care. They're also helping organizations anticipate changes in demand and create the sustainable procedures needed to confirm coverage. Additionally, get a rare lawyer's perspective on the standards that will be put forth for medical device manufacturers and pharmaceutical companies.

What are students learning in their first year of medical school? Does the curriculum coincide with the modern requirements of medicine today? Do they have quality healthcare as the centerpiece of coursework?

Chapter 7 takes readers to where it all starts: education. Significant partnerships between United States–based universities and professional organizations in other parts of the world exist to address challenges to the global state of public health. Some of them are focusing on innovation in medical school curricula, medical technology, mental health, and the cost of education.

Exclusive examples include Science Foundation Ireland, Harvard Catalyst, a groundbreaking department at the University of North Carolina that teaches nanomedicine and how to communicate its potential to the public, and the method of translational research that includes multidisciplined teams that form patient satisfaction programs from which students in medical school can learn.

Acts and legislation. Reform, regulations, and referendums. The government has assured high-quality, affordable healthcare for all Americans. Chapter 8 includes diverse views on how that guiding principle currently stacks up to the capacity of hospitals, the needs of physicians, and the roles of pharmaceutical companies, medical device manufacturers, and insurance companies. For hospitals and clinics, experts describe using legislation to limit internal industry politics, creating a system that incentivizes contracted physicians, employed physicians, nurses, and healthcare administration to find common ground. Other discussion points include how the government can play a role in mandating quality programs, healthy competition, care access, efficiency in work, and patient safety.

Last, Chapter 9 previews a few of the most fascinating technological advances to medicine still in development. This chapter proves how versatile, bizarre, expensive, experimental, and even fun the healthcare industry truly is.

Note that many individuals declined being interviewed for this book because of the heightened sensitivity around these topics or the red tape that the companies they work for would not cut. It's understandable. After all, we're talking about people's lives—from the middle-class suburbanites who can only afford medical attention for their children and not each other, to the farmer who sleeps in his truck because he chose blood pressure medicine over heating fuel. We pardon the ones who turned down interviews, but praise the ones who spoke their minds and helped this book come to be.

Chapter 1

Prevention and Personal Accountability

From an industrial engineer's perspective, the healthcare industry has such enormous potential for process improvement that those initiatives would mean employment for tens of thousands of Americans for decades. It is also the industry that is most vulnerable to unethical practices, untrained employees, inadequate facilities and equipment, and an outdated educational system. That's just the beginning!

It saddens me that our nation's healthcare industry represents chaos with so much distrust and uncertainty between patients and their doctors. The best is not being discussed among all the debating and deal signing in Congress. Perhaps equally important, the best is not known by individual patients.

But how do you convey just how process and the behind-the-scenes work in cost containment and efficiency lead to improving the fundamentals of patient care and experience? First, patients must play the often challenging role of day-to-day supervisor over their own personal habits and behavior.

In this day and age of employer-sponsored insurance benefits, those same employers are pulling out the red carpet to health and wellness programs, ranging from in-house yoga classes and memberships to the closest gym in the vicinity to hypnosis sessions to aid smokers in quitting the habit once and for all. Reasons for the corporate world's zealous participation in employees' well-being vary. From a business standpoint, employers who take an active role do save money when employees take care of themselves. Voluntary health risk assessments reveal the numbers when it comes to obesity, tobacco use, and stress, for example, which can easily correlate to sluggish worker performance, lagging productivity, and increased absence from the job.

These activities are helping people take responsibility for their own actions, or at least making them more aware of consequences, but the need for accountability as a component of the gigantic healthcare improvement equation is much more significant. It is increasingly apparent that our individual choices drive up healthcare costs, which are then incorporated into the cost of everything we consume.

Cost containment alone is such an overarching theme of our nation's healthcare industry that states such as Pennsylvania have implemented cost containment councils and countries such as Germany have enacted cost containment policies that distinguish sharply between hospital-based physicians and office-based physicians and separate fee scales. Additionally, many process improvement experts revolve their careers around containing cost. Consider the Institute of Industrial Engineers' official definition of *industrial engineering*:

> Industrial engineering is concerned with the design, improvement and installation of integrated systems of people, materials, information, equipment and energy. It draws upon specialized knowledge and skill in the mathematical, physical, and social sciences together with the principles and methods of engineering analysis and design, to specify, predict, and evaluate the results to be obtained from such systems.

Further, duties of these efficiency and productivity champions include reducing costs associated with new technologies; instilling the ability to do more with less; making work safer, faster, easier, and more rewarding; and establishing efficient and more profitable business practices.

When inflated healthcare costs are exposed after a "process intervention," the insurance companies, physicians, hospitals, or government departments are called to assume responsibility in some way. In essence, personal lifestyle choice is also a staple component of the struggle to contain cost and improve health, and it must be present in the conversation.

Case Study of the Cost of Personal Choice

Ever taste something so sweet, your head left your shoulders and spiraled up to the ceiling in delight? Strawberry, vanilla, or milk chocolate frosting, the sweetness is so heavenly it tickles your tongue for long after you've spooned it into your mouth. My friend was hooked at the age of six, when her mother allowed her to scoop as much chocolate frosting out of the can as she wanted. Her mother had already topped a birthday cake, so the extra had no other purpose than shameless sugar intake. So began my friend's love of sweets.

Years later, her first job would be at a bakery, where she designed a kitchen full of cakes each morning. She spooned so much icing into her mouth the sugar twirled her into a light-headed stupor more than a few times for sure. Then there was the ice cream parlor, where eating a five-scoop peanut butter sundae accounted for break time each day.

This anecdote has a purpose other than sparking hunger. It's a true tale of how, at a young age, someone can assume poor eating habits and continue through adulthood married to these habits that have the potential to result in dire consequences—diabetes, hypertension, and obesity, to name a few.

My friend remained in the food industry for years, engulfed in the preparation of Italian, French, Spanish, Southwestern, Southern, and Indian foods. However, fortunately, her love of food didn't send her body into a tailspin of health ailments because she became proactive about nutrition and exercise, relaxation, and mental well-being in her twenties. Both of her parents had ultimately died of a lethal combination of addictions, namely, food, alcohol, and filterless cigarettes.

Countless writings and clinical trials over the years have told us that stronger well-being, one and the same with looking and feeling better, results from nature's infinite offerings, the smorgasbord of balanced meals created all over the planet, the body's remarkable capabilities, and the mind's horizons.

So why is our nation so poor in good health and abundant in diseases that are preventable?

Improvements in health must be embraced with some sense of excitement and dedication if they are to be permanent. The life cycle of improvement begins with the individual person, spans all healthcare workers and facilities involved in the care of that person, and ends with the government, which oversees our nation's healthcare system.

According to the Centers for Disease Control and Prevention (CDC), most people do not engage in healthy behaviors that can prevent obesity. Note that in 2003, direct costs attributable to obesity amounted to approximately $75 billion, with annual hospital costs related to obesity more than tripling over the past two decades. Cardiovascular disease and diabetes also knocked on the door of these patients, including Anya, an example mentioned below.

In the coming chapters, we define systems thinking and suggest solutions for our nation's health systems. In getting to the root of a system, you must examine every part of the sum—in this case, living and breathing people. The examples are not meant to cast judgment on any one population; the information merely provides context.

Industrial engineering is comprised of case studies in which to benchmark for process improvement. This practice begins here.

Let me give you an example of someone who didn't take personal accountability for her reactions until near death—a person I will call Anya Hanes, a high school teacher in Los Angeles, California. What you should know is that prescription pills for high blood pressure, lipid disorders, thyroid issues, diabetes, sleep apnea, and high cholesterol lined the 52-year-old's medicine cabinet, and she paid about $350 a month for these prescriptions for nearly *15 years*. Anya was not eligible for assistance from Medi-Cal, the state of California's Medicaid program. But as you learn what Anya's conscious habits consisted of for all those years, you decide if she—if poor—should have received the assistance.

Having agreed to be interviewed and participate in a weight loss book, Anya painted the portrait of her health as the following: a diet overstuffed with chocolate doughnuts, pasta, fries, and ham sandwiches. Two doughnuts for breakfast, a plate of penne pasta with cream sauce for lunch, and fries accompanied by a ham and cheese sandwich for dinner equaled Anya's frequent calorie intake: over 2,300. The total doesn't include a cup of coffee with table sugar, two cans of soda, the occasional bread basket with butter, and 2 teaspoons of mayonnaise: another 550–700 calories, confirms Nutrition Data.

Considering her schedule at a tough inner city school, one might understand how weight loss got pushed back on Anya's priority list to some degree, but for 15 years?

"The stress I was under to keep very troubled, discouraged teenagers to stay positive superseded my interest in taking care of my own self properly … until I was in severely poor health," she said. "I had relied on doctors, fitness magazines, food labels, and calorie amounts to set unrealistic goals for me that I knew I wouldn't keep, but it was nice to daydream about the results sometimes."

Does this sound like someone taking personal responsibility before entering the doors to our healthcare systems for help?

Ultimately, Anya did change her lifestyle and lost more than 70 pounds in the first year of practicing newfound habits. Subsequently, a year's worth of consultations with a bariatrics medical director cost $4,000, which Medi-Cal did pay for. By the time she had enrolled in a wellness program, Anya had lost her teaching job, along with hundreds of others from the same school district. In 2007, unfortunately while improving her physical health, Anya filed bankruptcy. She was among the 62 percent of Americans who filed due to excessive medical expenses.

As you will see, the themes of employer-sponsored, state-sponsored, or insurance-sponsored wellness programs, personalized medicine, care ethics, the Obama administration's health reform, and many other topics in the coming chapters of this book all touch Anya's story. One individual.

The Expert Is In: The Number 1 Improvement: Teach Prevention and Wellness

Enter another perspective on this type of story. Dr. Gez Agolli is the managing director of Progressive Medical Centers of America based in Atlanta. Beyond being a board-certified naturopath and possessing a healthcare management certification, his education combines degrees in naturopathic medicine, nutrition, herbology, and healthcare administration.

"Our current healthcare symptom is in crisis," urged Agolli. "We are in a crisis because we as a nation spend over 18 percent of our annual GNP on healthcare. Yet we are one of the most unhealthiest nations compared to other industrialized nations as a whole. Obesity, cancer, heart disease and diabetes, just to name a few, are on an all-time high. Why? There are multifactoral reasons. However, the number 1 improvement in healthcare that must be made is teaching prevention and wellness; not to just talk about, but set up, programs and make our citizens accountable. It starts from the top!"

Progressive Medical Centers is unique in that it is a state-of-the-art integrative medical facility utilizing the latest advancements in lab technology. It has the ability to diagnose a patient's current biochemistry and toxic elements in his or her body tissue through blood, saliva, urine, hair, and stool, explains Agolli.

"This process gets to the root cause of a disease. Once diagnosed, we have the latest innovative tools to treat them effectively, allowing the patient an opportunity to heal from the inside out. Progressive utilizes hyperbaric oxygen, infrared technology, bioelectrical medicine, individualized nutrition, nutritional IVs, and customized fitness routines in our state-of-the-art fitness center. Progressive stands out because not only do we get to the root cause of disease, but we individualize a treatment plan involving wellness, diet, detoxification, and proper supplementation while treating infections when necessary, balancing the body's electrical system, and treating pain with noninvasive methods."

Agolli's medical team stands out because workers are trained to listen to their patients' needs and set up a plan for wellness. Placating symptoms through prescriptions that may have severe side effects is not an option at Progressive. "The only time we will use a prescription is to treat severe infections, and that will be for a short period of time," said Agolli.

Though Progressive does integrate conventional medicine in specific situations, its very nature works against the grain of traditional medical practices and hospitals that have been the heart of the nation's soaring healthcare costs. More specifically, the center's expertise seeks to

- Reduce reliance on pharmaceuticals
- Relieve side effects caused by pharmaceuticals
- Eliminate the need for surgery
- Avoid hospital stays

- ■ Treat the root cause of a person's illness, rather than just suppress symptoms
- ■ Conduct more in-depth testing to get to the source of a person's illness

Does this road map to better health sound more proactive? It eliminates waste in spending, time, and labor while somehow giving the patient more control than he or she may have had over his or her own body before walking through the center's doors. Agolli does acknowledge that "conventional Western medicine is superior in situations that call for trauma intervention, surgery, or antibiotic therapy for acute infection, but chronic diseases and conditions are not easily treated by the same system."

Dr. Robert Zarr is a well-known pediatrician based in Washington, D.C. In between seeing patients during 2009, Zarr could be found leading healthcare reform rallies as co-chairman of the Physicians for a National Health Program D.C. chapter. He is a staunch advocate for children's wellness with a focus on quality improvement initiatives on topics that we don't often hear of from the medical world: asthma management, injury prevention, literacy promotion, breastfeeding awareness, and tuberculosis screening.

"I have the perspective that healthcare access is a basic right, but you must take personal responsibility for the health choices that you make also," Zarr said. "There are many influencers of health. We see every walk of life in our practice— the working class, homeless, those that cannot walk the streets of their neighborhoods safely after work or eat right most of the time. Exercise becomes difficult in certain lifestyles. The choice of whether to eat dinner or pay a copay to find out if you have a cancerous mole is a disturbing reality. Healthcare is a fundamental human right."

Why do we go from the basics that Zarr suggests to more complex issues like personalized medicine in our dialogue and our legislation? Because personalized medicine is rooted in the information about an individual patient. The subject and consequences of either applying or not applying the methods available to us aren't purposely being hidden behind closed doors for the wealthy. However, we don't have a history of proactively seeking the information and probing our doctors for options.

Age, lifestyle, genes, and overall health play a role in each person's care, so why are we all taking the same medicines and embarking on the same therapeutic methods and surgeries?

To understand the full reality of the state of health we *could* have, as Zarr points out, we must deal with our personal business of diet, exercise, and education. Based on the disturbing statistics involving diabetes and obesity, for instance, some of us have become passing ships in the night to our own well-being.

That said, it's urgent that we also get ahead of the curve on more sophisticated initiatives that Congress is acting on— medical channels that have the power to effect all of us at some point in our lives, such as stem cell research.

Personalized medicine includes the aspects of stem cell therapy that have already been used for treating some cancers and are being closely examined in the treatment of heart attack victims and certain tissue repairs. To debunk any myths that have been spewed in political and religious arguments, let's consider the basic premise of stem cell research and treatment.

According to Stephen Schimpff, MD, FACP, in his book *The Future of Medicine*, the key characteristics of stem cells are that they can replicate themselves and can become mature cells that make up the body. *Embryonic stem cells* can become any of the body's approximately 200 types of cells (liver, lung, etc.), and they have the capacity to divide or replicate indefinitely. *Adult stem cells* are found in adults, newborns, and children. They are found in many organs and tissues, will divide multiple times in tissue culture, but not so indefinitely as embryonic stem cells.

Spinal cord injuries, Parkinson's disease, juvenile diabetes, and Alzheimer's are among the medical conditions at the heart of stem cell research. Things are moving rapidly in the stem cell research field now, after decades of largely private research, so it is most certainly one area of personalized medicine to stay abreast of. Since personalized medicine is also a medical model that emphasizes the systematic use of information, or collected data, about an individual to choose, lengthen, or optimize preventative and therapeutic care, efficiency and effectiveness are innate.

Junell Scheeres is the president of LS2 Performance Solutions, LLC, which delivers comprehensive lean Six Sigma life cycle consulting services designed to support an organization's performance improvement program. She has specialized in healthcare settings for more than 25 years, having conducted projects resulting in quicker turnaround times, less waiting, lower costs, higher efficiency, and improved patient care in hospitals across the United States.

"Healthcare treatment is traditionally reactive versus proactive," Scheeres said. "As a science, medical practice is responsive to observation, intervention, and then confirmation of changes. Preventative care relies on the value system of the patient, not so much the funding of the care. With the advent of incentivized financial benefit through flexible health savings accounts, there is a potential for patients to apply their healthcare dollars towards prevention, if so inclined.

"I think behaviorally, we are mostly in denial of the risks and consequences of our values-based choices that put our health at risk, and are more inclined towards dealing with a known episode rather than take the time to be proactive in our care, unless a compelling significant emotional event alters that inclination (like a strong family history, or the illness of a friend or 'hero')."

Having written about this same concept in two different articles over the last few years, one specifically in the June 2013 edition of *Industrial Engineer* magazine, published by the Institute of Industrial Engineers, too often I find that we address challenges in a most reactive manner. A problem arises, we address it. We spend very precious time—and dollars—to derive some sort of solution to minimize or eliminate the impact of this problem. Obviously, responding reactively to some situations is almost inevitable; it doesn't mean it always has to be that way. For example, the concept of root cause analysis (or as I like to refer to it, RCA) is a highly used, and often very effective, method for identifying a particular cause of a problem, as derived from its "symptoms." A healthcare professional—or any for that matter—is generally not aware of the challenge, and hence the need for something to support the identification of the cause. But, what if we could be aware before anything could ever happen? We can! Although we talk about this in Chapter 2, this is critical given the times we are in. Thinking predictively by turning some of these methods "on its head" will allow for the understanding of potential challenges and uncertainty as early as possible to minimize, or completely negate, the impact of potential challenges the future may hold. This requires thinking about how organizational objectives align to patient demand, uncertainty (or risk), and patient care to achieve some level of prevention (Figure 1.1).

With that understood, we need facilities like Progressive Medical Centers of America, physician-advocates like Dr. Robert Zarr, and healthcare engineers like Junell Scheeres to provide the full spectrum of expertise that American medicine requires for its best capabilities. There is simply more to addressing healthcare challenges than immediately responding to a particular problem at a given time and place.

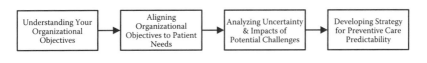

Figure 1.1   Predictive thinking for organizational problem solving.

Also, getting past medical jargon and highly technical terminology, we cannot afford to be in the dark on information about golden opportunities that areas such as personalized medicine offer. Above all this, however, we must realize that the manic variation in care that we receive first depends on our own actions.

Critical Q&A

Why does most medicine still emphasize proximate causes of diseases rather than the prevention, diagnosis, and treatment?

Our system pays much more handsomely to treat disease than it does to prevent it. Our system's reimbursement schedule is tilted heavily toward procedures. Typically, preventive medicine requires no procedures and few diagnostic tests; there is little money for providers to make doing this type of medicine. Therefore, most doctors, hospitals, and other providers pursue treatments for established diseases.

—James Rickert, MD, orthopedic surgeon

What drives practice is what's billable. You have to generate revenue through a practice. Some physicians are salary based at HMOs like Kaiser, community health centers, and hospitals. The goal is to see more patients and do more things in less time. Counseling children on obesity does not make a lot of money. Fewer people are doing preventative tasks. To our credit, pediatricians do a lot of screening even when it's not necessary. But it can be like an assembly line, getting every patient through screening within 15 minutes. There is an enormous shortage of primary care doctors in this country.

—Robert Zarr, medical director of Pediatrics, Unity Healthcare, Inc.

What issues are often skirted, ignored, or hidden behind jargon when it comes to health systems?

One of the first that comes to mind is flow or throughput. Healthcare workers often have the misconception that things cannot be done well and quickly, that one can either do something fast or with high quality, but not both at the same time. The second is the patient focus. We often hear "we are here for the patient," but you still see processes designed for the convenience of the technical staff or physicians rather than the patient. For example, in order to get chest x-rays on the chart for physician rounds, we need to start at 5 a.m. It is hard to reconcile "we are here for the patient" with waking someone up at 5 a.m. to get a chest x-ray so a physician can see it when they decide to make rounds.

—Charles Debusk, VP Performance and Process Improvement, Universal Health Services

Chapter 2

System Says ...

Whether it's a medical device or an automobile, practices and processes form the bond between products and the level of quality consumers receive from them. Before programs were put into place to help protect consumers, quality was a natural expectation, an unspoken promise by a manufacturer. The rules of quality are coveted among manufacturing companies, so why not among all healthcare facilities?

To look at an industry, starting with a system as the foundation for it, is to truly see the full circumference. You then see the resources involved in running the system and what the processes are. From there, you see where improvements can be made.

Before we enter one of the most complicated systems in existence today—the U.S. healthcare industry—briefly step into a manufacturing setting, where you'll notice tools and strategies that contribute to the journey to business excellence. At any given time, if one tool fails, production could be set back by many days and dollars, impacting customer service, distribution, marketing, transportation, and inventory.

There are available short-term solutions: double shifts, decreased bonuses, shortened lead times. However, there are sustainable solutions, and implementing them requires a different finesse within a leadership league of its own.

Following the Right Leader

Studies in motivation, such as the Hawthorne experiments at Western Electric Hawthorne Works in the 1920s, examined the impact of work conditions on employee productivity. While the exercise was prompted by questions on the physical lighting in the work environment, variables affecting productivity stacked up, including fatigue, monotony, humidity, and stressful schedules. In the end, the spotlight was on the leadership's ability to engage employees in the improvement process by listening to their concerns, showing empathy, and introducing subtle yet favorable changes to their workdays.

Elton Mayo, the professor who conducted the experiments at this manufacturing plant, came to the following conclusions, which have been referenced in countless leadership books:

- An individual's aptitude alone is not a predictor of job performance; social factors are strong influencers.
- Relationships between leaders and employees influence how the workers carry out assigned tasks.
- Teams arrive at their own norms and expectations for their workdays, regardless of what's outlined in the operations manual.
- The worker is a human being whose attitude and ability are conditioned by social demands from both inside and outside of the workplace.
- The need for belonging and recognition is even more important than the tools and environment in which the work is conducted.

Amazingly, many of the process improvement tools and leadership strategies do and will continue to apply to patient care. Just as we have seen the applicability of root cause analysis (RCA)—a very common tool to many industries—all industries share common structures in finance, operations, and subsequently systems and processes to produce some particular good or service. The glaring difference in that one failed tool is that a person, not a product, may be at stake. The process improvement experts who cross into healthcare settings will do so with an acute sensitivity to the aggressive, intense goals associated with this specific industry, and they are to be commended for that specialization.

There are a number of models that contribute to the type of systems engineering that applies to healthcare. Because of the high-risk environments that emergency rooms and operating theaters are, this chapter illustrates the ones being frequently practiced in hospitals. Note that because of the high rate of results associated with these programs, they are slowly being carried on workers' shoulders into mental health facilities, community health centers, and prehospital emergency settings as well.

First, the million-dollar question is: *How do you create an organizational culture that is receptive to lean thinking, specifically in a complex healthcare environment?*

"The classic model is to create a sense of urgency, develop a future vision that benefits all (patients, staff, organization), and then work persistently to make it happen," noted Chuck Noon, PhD, a professor in the Department of Management at the University of Tennessee.

Noon's research and teaching interests focus on operations management, business modeling, and decision analysis. As part of its Learning and Innovation Community on Operational and Clinical Improvement in the emergency department, the Institute of Healthcare Improvement sought Noon's expertise for a lean simulation training session that five hospital teams participated in.

Both physicians and nurses participated in a flurry of activities that represented a day in the emergency department, complete with mock exam rooms, labs, reception and triage areas, supply closets, and other components of a 12-bed, 14-exam bay emergency department. Attendees often switched roles during the exercise, which was designed to process wait times and complaints. Noon and a colleague led a post-activity discussion on how lean methods could have improved staff performance and patient experiences.

"As easy as it sounds, this [harmony] is extremely challenging due to the distinct characteristics of healthcare," Noon explained. He adds:

> For example, there's not much sense of external threat ("If we perform poorly, it's not like they're going to close us"), and overall incentives are not very direct (reimbursements are mostly the same for good or bad quality). The highest level of redundancy and ineffectiveness in an emergency department is in the information gathering (often front-end) processes, especially for low-acuity patients.
>
> Inefficiency is often the result of a tendency to use more beds than really needed. This creates excessive complexity and waste in the form of movement. What's needed is, in the true spirit of lean, a process perspective across the entire healthcare value chain, including the payers. The interdependency between service providers, payers and patients is complex, and without an overall perspective, it defaults to a state of local optimization for each player, and thereby global inefficiency for the system in total. When all sides act as if they are on the same team, real gains can be identified, implemented, and sustained.

What gains does Noon refer to exactly? The Institute for Healthcare Improvement adheres to an ambitious set of goals entitled the "No Needless List," which is a solid measurement of continual progress toward bold objectives and changing the lives of patients:

■ No needless deaths
■ No needless pain or suffering

- No helplessness in those served or serving
- No unwanted waiting
- No waste
- No one left out

When TOC Is Better than TLC

One form of systems thinking behind the glory of process improvement models is the theory of constraints (TOC), which was developed by Eliyahu Goldratt, a physicist and economist who has educated executive teams from many of the world's largest corporations, including General Motors, AT&T, Procter & Gamble, and NV Philips. Goldratt is also the author of *The Goal*, an unconventional business book centered on TOC that has sold in the millions.

The theory of constraints is a form of systems thinking that looks at an enterprise as a complete and complex system where any number of constituent parts interact with one another; if a constraint is anything that limits a system from achieving higher performance versus its goal, then every system must have at least one constraint or limiting factor. Identifying and managing the constraint then becomes the nucleus for change, so starting with the recognition of the constraint begins the difference between a *problem* and an *opportunity*.

Additionally, TOC encompasses tools defined as "thinking processes" and the sequence in which they are used. The tools enable people to analyze their systems to determine what to change and how to change it.

The Goldratt Institute defines a constraint as "anything that prevents the system from achieving more of its goal." Further, there are many ways that constraints can show up, but a core principle within TOC is that there are not tens or hundreds of constraints. There is at least one and at most a few in any given system.

Constraints can be internal or external to the system. An internal constraint is in evidence when the market demands more from the system than it can deliver. If this is the case, then the focus of the organization should be on discovering that constraint and following the five focusing steps to open it up (and potentially remove it). An external constraint exists when the system can produce more than the market will bear. If this is the case, then the organization should focus on mechanisms to create more demand for its products or services.

The true measurement of success is how well a system performs relative to the goal. (Critics of our nation's healthcare system would argue that the goal has switched from making a person walk or taking the patient off a respirator to making enough profit to keep a faulty system going.) Within a goal, there are three operational performance measurements: throughput, inventory, and operating expense.

Throughput is defined as the rate at which the system generates money through sales and is represented as sales minus "totally variable" cost; however, output that is not sold is inventory. Inventory is defined as all the money invested in things the system intends to sell: raw material, work in process, unsold finished products, tools, building, and equipment. In the following examples that support TOC, patients can fall into the category of inventory.

Lastly, operating expense is defined as the money the system spends in turning inventory into throughput: wages, salaries, bills, and interest payments.

Now, back to those goals! The Institute of Medicine has established six aims for healthcare to satisfy: safety, effectiveness, efficiency, timeliness, family-centered focus, and equity. Keep in mind that the aims target everyone involved in the realm of care, from the staff to the patients they tend to.

Each aim can be considered in terms of size and weight of importance, followed by a series of questions as a guidepost for items to improve.

Safety

Healthcare facilities play host to numerous health and safety issues associated with everything from biological hazards, potential chemical and drug exposures, waste anesthetic gas exposures, respiratory hazards, ergonomic hazards from lifting and repetitive tasks to laser hazards, hazards associated with laboratories, and radioactive material and x-ray hazards. As the Occupational Safety and Health Administration explains, some of these potential chemical exposures include formaldehyde, used for preservation of specimens for pathology, and paracetic acid, used for sterilization, for example.

In addition to the medical staff, large healthcare facilities employ a wide variety of trades that have health and safety hazards associated with them. These include mechanical maintenance, medical equipment maintenance, housekeeping, food service, building and grounds maintenance, laundry, and administrative staff. Dentistry safety, disaster management, healthcare bioterrorism, malpractice, and infection control are also common areas of focus for instituting expansive and measurable programs.

Healthcare waste management policies and plans should include provision for the continuous monitoring of workers' health and safety to ensure that correct handling, treatment, storage, and disposal procedures are being followed. Essential occupational health and safety measures include the following:

■ Proper training of workers
■ Provision of equipment and clothing for personal protection
■ Establishment of an effective occupational health program that includes immunization, post-exposure prophylactic treatment, and medical surveillance

Training in health and safety should ensure that workers know of and understand the potential risks associated with healthcare waste, the value of immunization against viral hepatitis B, and the importance of consistent use of personal protection equipment.

As you can see, safety is of the utmost concern in health systems. In some cases, to not practice safety may be the difference between life and death.

Patient safety practices must be at the heart of a fully functioning health system, and they're defined by processes or structures whose applications reduce the probability of adverse events resulting from exposure to the public healthcare realm across a range of diseases and procedures. Many programs focus on hospitals as the epicenter because of the level of risk involved virtually in every corridor. Other sites of care with high risk are ambulances and nursing homes.

In spearheading patient safety programs, process improvement consultants typically have experience in leadership engagement, clinical practices as they relate to a certain environment, and patient education. For healthcare, in particular, performance excellence and safety are intertwined—you cannot have one without the other.

Safety programs will typically include the following:

- Top-down leadership—clear, consistent expectations
- Bottom-up ownership and employee engagement
- Training and a general education plan
- Action plans and corresponding measures
- Visual communication
- Standards and procedures (and documentation of)
- Benchmarking and goals
- Audits
- A reward system
- A safety culture embedded in a department (or hopefully, organization)

Effectiveness

The delivery of healthcare from each channel includes how it is funded or paid for, how services are delivered, what services and benefits are provided, how the various parts are coordinated, and what data and information are needed for it to function effectively as a system. Obviously, hospitals are included. Public and private organizations are included. Nursing homes and free clinics are included. Psychiatric hospitals are included. But what is the actual "system" that they function from?

Some of the experts in this book openly expressed frustration because they don't consider the nationwide entanglement of thousands of different channels operating on different planes an actual system. Are practices and procedures logical? Are they effective for the patient? Are funded activities necessary and safe? Are the data collected helping nurses, doctors, administrators, policy makers, and stakeholders make good decisions? Are Medicaid and Medicare running properly?

Learning how to provide leadership within an organization through continuing medical education may help to field some of this information to the appropriate channels. Building teams with the greater purpose of nurturing strong relationships with patients must be accentuated with being informed of important information and being able to decipher how that information will help the patient.

Donald Campbell, MD, senior vice president of physician leadership at WellStar Health System in Atlanta, explained, "The breadth of continuing medical education topics is so broad that it would be very hard to choose any aspect as most important. The information that physicians need to safely and effectively practice medicine changes at a rate that it is impossible for practicing physicians to keep up with. Systems in electronic health records (EHRs) are now being put into place that will make it easier for physicians to choose treatments according to best practices. The behavior that is needed is for physicians to accept this new information and incorporate it into their practice, rather than dismissing it because of their reluctance to change. I would prioritize training and education that would best equip physicians to use all of the existing channels of information available to them to bring the latest evidence-based practice to their patients."

Efficiency

It must be defined, measured, and used to achieve specific goals. Even the Academy of Health insists that measurement of efficiency is challenging due to the lack of definition of terms, lack of an agreed upon framework of efficiency, differential access to data, and unresolved technical issues, such as sampling methods. Costs and quality must correlate. Redundancy must be spared for accuracy.

There are numerous types of efficiency in healthcare. Should we focus on it in terms of financial cost or the care of a patient versus society in general, as many physicians view it? What elements of healthcare should be valued most? Additionally, perspective or perception plays a key role in the version of efficiency at work at any given time. Consumers, providers, process improvement engineers, stakeholders, insurance purchasers, and payers typically have a different point of view. For certain, this contributes to the fragmentation in health systems around the world today.

For project initiatives, in general, the aim is to attach measurement and improvement wherever the concept of efficiency can help the most.

Paul O'Quinn is a performance improvement consultant at Carilion Clinic, a multiunit health system that has been designated a magnet status hospital by the American Nurses Credentialing System. He insists that the United States can no longer afford to attempt to make improvements using outdated approaches.

"A barrier to cost reduction for many healthcare systems is an inefficient and ineffective approach to process improvement," said O'Quinn. "I like to use the analogy of assembling a TV stand. Which method is likely to produce a better assembly—relying solely on your intuitive mechanical ability or following the instructions provided by the manufacturer? Just as there is a structured approach for assembling a TV stand, there is a structured approach for process improvement. If we follow such an approach, we end up with a better outcome. We often make the mistake of relying solely on intuition. In the case of the TV stand, we end up with leftover parts. In the case of process improvement, we end up with improvement initiatives that drag out for months (sometimes years) and fail to produce the desired results."

However, this should not be considered a limitation to creativeness. A process improvement approach—or any analytical method or technique—should be the starting point of your creative process for improving a particular system or process. Time and time again, I've watched so-called improvement experts use the same tools and methods day in and day out on very different problems. While it may work in some cases, do not be limited to what you have used on a prior engagement or have learned in academic coursework or training. Use that as a starting point, and follow a structured approach, but do not be afraid to adjust as necessary to achieve a faster, and same or higher-quality, result.

In another article for the Institute of Industrial Engineers, I wrote about creativity and how all too often we tend to use the same, and often outdated, methods to solve very different and more complex methods. Seeing lean Six Sigma practitioners continue to apply the same SIPOC (suppliers, inputs, process(es), outputs, customers) framework (Figure 2.1) to every system challenge drove me crazy. It is a starting point, but let your brainpower drive its tailoring or redevelopment for the particular challenge you seek to address. For example, using a SIPOC to identify the system/process

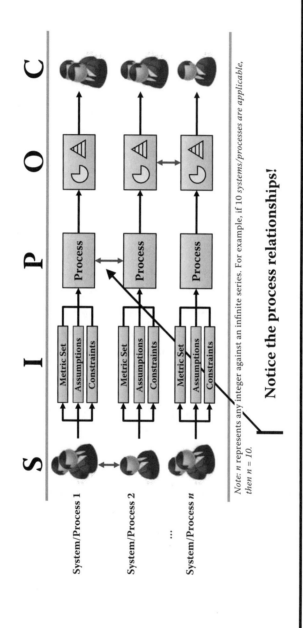

Figure 2.1 Identifying relationships through use of a SIPOC model.

relationships from one category to the next allows for a greater understanding of the system/process, but more importantly, the impact of potential improvements on other systems/processes. In many cases I have been requested to support efforts that require fixing for what should have already been fixed. The problem was not the effort put into the project by the team, but rather the application of an approach that simply was not optimal.

As O'Quinn mentioned, following an approach, you'll end up with a better outcome, but let's shoot for an *optimal* outcome, and one that considers the entire system of systems or system of processes and the relationships from one to another. That to include the impact of one improvement option over another as analyzed against key metrics, such as performance, cost, schedule, and risk.

Timeliness

Efficiency and timeliness go hand and hand. To give an immediate example of this aim's challenges and successes and a lesson in efficiency, consider an award-winning process initiative that began in April 2002. Cincinnati Children's received a $1.9 million grant from the Robert Wood Johnson Foundation to participate in Pursuing Perfection: Raising the Bar for Healthcare Performance. In April 2004, Cincinnati Children's received an additional $300,000 for its goals.

In at least two of its concentration areas, the Robert Wood Johnson Foundation further validates the importance of personal accountability as a role in improvement. The foundation is the nation's largest philanthropy devoted exclusively to health and healthcare. It concentrates its grant making in four goal areas: to ensure that all Americans have access to basic healthcare at reasonable cost; to improve care and support for people with chronic health conditions; to promote healthy communities and lifestyles; and to reduce the personal, social, and economic harm caused by substance abuse—tobacco, alcohol, and illicit drugs.

Pursuing Perfection is a response to two reports from the Institute of Medicine that questioned the safety, quality, efficiency, effectiveness, and fairness of the nation's healthcare system. Pursuing Perfection was intended to be a catalyst for rapid, transformational change, and participants produce compelling examples of how healthcare organizations can significantly improve. Cincinnati Children's is the only pediatric facility among seven organizations chosen for the grant.

The project team at Cincinnati Children's reported the following improvements on its website:

- Wait time for same-day surgery patients was reduced from 67 to 35 minutes using an expedited outpatient process.
- Instrument processing time for general surgery was reduced by 51 percent, allowing for more timely surgery.
- Ongoing training is being conducted for all surgery staff to learn how to better involve families in caring for children.
- New surgery education packets have been designed for patients and their families.
- Hospital admission rates for several common childhood illnesses were reduced by 15 percent.
- Adolescents hospitalized with cystic fibrosis customize their own inpatient schedules to meet their individual needs.
- The Liver Care Center developed a secure website that gives patients online access to their own medical information. The site provides information patients and families need to be active, informed members of the healthcare team.
- The Cystic Fibrosis (CF) Team implemented new protocols to change the way Cincinnati Children's manages weight gain in CF patients. After only 90 days, the team saw significant improvements in a number of patients.

■ An improved discharge planning process has been implemented, allowing families to go home sooner after the
child reaches discharge criteria.
■ Parking spaces just for same-day surgery patients are now
available.
■ The average wait time for infants with a fever of uncertain source to receive antibiotic treatment after arriving
in the emergency department has been reduced by over
53 percent.

Cincinnati Children's Hospital received the 2006 American
Hospital Association–McKesson Quest for Quality Prize, which
is presented annually to an organization that achieves the
Institute of Medicine's six quality aims. Cincinnati Children's
was one of seven healthcare organizations, and the only
pediatric center, to receive this honor.

This project was initiated with the extraordinary goal of
transforming the healthcare system in America. With this positive momentum and volume of information available to the
public, there are many similar initiatives taking place across
the country—and not just in reputable, large hospitals with
infinite resources.

A Different Strain of Lean

In rural areas, time considerations could also include the
door-to-door distance between a home in a rugged area of the
South and the entranceway to a small facility like Meadows
Regional Medical Center in Vidalia, Georgia. With only one
healthcare facility in proximity, you can't be sure how many
residents will be in the emergency room with an allergic
reaction or diabetic coma, literally dying to be seen.

Theses worries prompted funding from the Georgia Rural
Economic Development Center in order for experts to conduct
a three-day lean overview workshop and value stream

mapping event with emergency nursing staff, an ER physician, the radiology director, the laboratory manager, and business office staff. Georgia Institute of Technology, which is home to the largest industrial engineering program of its kind in the United States, took the opportunity to send a multidisciplined team to the site.

With assistance from the institute, the hospital implemented lean manufacturing principles after the average length of stay in the ER regularly exceeded 200 minutes.

Issues with bottlenecking, turnaround times, decreased satisfaction, and overworked nurses were marked by patient complaints by the hour on some days until lean specialists began the hospital's transformation in June 2005.

The lean team at Meadows developed 44 action items for reducing the time needed to admit, treat, and discharge noncritical ER patients. Forty-one percent of the items were determined to be low cost and high impact, spanning seven categories: 5S and visual controls, cross-training, equipment, hospital procedures, patient information, general procedures, and staffing.

Changes made by the hospital included standardizing mobile supply stations; labeling racks, trays, and drawers; installing a color-coded flag system outside patient rooms; issuing patients red allergy armbands to alert medical staff; and adding a holding area for patients who need to see a doctor but who don't need a room.

The hospital also implemented the T-System, a software program that shows staff who is in the waiting room, who needs an x-ray, and who can be put into a room or a wheel-chair. The T-System also documents length of stay, lab tests ordered, physician and nurse assigned to the patient, and discharge disposition, as well as patient name, room number, and prior ER visits.

Interestingly, the T-System software solutions were founded by actual emergency medicine physicians in 1996 because of the need for process improvement in emergency departments.

After practicing medicine for 35 years, Woodrow Gandy, MD, and Robert Langdon, MD, wanted to create a system focused on five process upgrades: predictable (yes!), efficient work flow, ease of clinical documentation, incomparable work content, improved patient outcomes, and solutions to rely on long term.

According to T-System, today, more than 1,800 civilian and military emergency departments in the United States, Puerto Rico, Australia, and around the world partner with T-System to improve work flow, charge capture, quality of patient care, and staff satisfaction.

Lean is certainly not a new concept. From the simple transformation of even the most minor of processes to much more complex challenges, lean concepts simply allow you to identify challenges (for example, via RCA or some other tool) and develop solutions that may promote greater efficiency while maintaining the same—or better—level of quality. All you need is an understanding of what a better end state may be, and what lean tools may allow you to begin creating a solution to the problem. Whether you leverage free webinars, Google searches, or buy a text or two from the local bookstore, there are plenty of avenues for gaining greater insight into lean.

Family-Centered Focus

It is critical for a hospital to include the patient's family in making key decisions surrounding the care. All facilities should have a system in place to collect feedback based on their approaches to care, and they can use this informative to improve existing quality programs and overall satisfaction. The voice of the customer—in the case of healthcare service, the patient and family members—is absolutely critical to the mission of the hospital in saving lives and healing patients. This is just one aspect of family-centered care.

The word *family* refers to two or more persons who are related in any way—biologically, legally, or emotionally. Patients and families define their families. It's important to clarify the term because in the past, parents and legal spouses only possessed the rights to be included in this circle of decision making. In the patient- and family-centered approach, the definition of family, as well as the degree of the family's involvement in healthcare, is determined by the patient, provided that he or she is developmentally mature and competent to do so.

The term *family-centered* is in no way intended to remove control from patients who are competent to make decisions concerning their own healthcare. In pediatrics, particularly with infants and young children, family members are defined by the patient's parents or guardians.

The Institute for Patient- and Family-Centered Care also defines its focus as an innovative approach to the planning, delivery, and evaluation of healthcare that is grounded in mutually beneficial partnerships among healthcare providers, patients, and families. The core aspects of the care include respect and dignity, information sharing, participation, and collaboration. It also differentiates between family-centered focus (again, the Institute of Medicine's aim) and family-centered care:

> In family-focused care, professionals often provide care from the position of an "expert"—assessing the patient and family, recommending a treatment or intervention, and creating a plan for the family to follow. They do things to and for the patient and family, regarding the family as the "unit of intervention." Family-centered care, by contrast, is characterized by a collaborative approach to caregiving and decision making. Each party respects the knowledge, skills, and experience that the other brings to healthcare encounters. The family and healthcare team collaboratively assess the needs and development of the treatment plan.

Equity

Fairness in healthcare is such a heated topic that it was presumably the basis for a man's finger being bitten off by a counterprotester during a healthcare rally in 2009. Let's be clear that there is a bizarre humor to this, but perhaps the underlining reason for the outburst between two grown men was the deep-rooted anger associated with helplessness and the fear that comes with the unknown.

The healthcare rallies that took place before the Obama administration enacted the Affordable Care Act. Numerous aspects of equity in healthcare were brought to the surface—some for the first time—because of the ripe political and socioeconomic climate.

Most of us want to see fairness in the way that we allocate our healthcare resources and fairness in the way that we fund our system. For the uninsured and underinsured, it's not clear how equity applies at any given time. Additionally, there are categories to define among the uninsured and the underinsured. As of 2011, there were approximately 11.5 million illegal immigrants residing in the United States. Should equity apply to this population sampling in the same way that it applies to the millions of Americans who may be temporarily unemployed and uninsured at any given time?

For employers that are struggling to keep the doors open but still offer a group healthcare plan to both retain good employees and meet tax incentives, equity may seem convoluted or questionable. For other purchasers of healthcare, including the government and more affluent individuals, the adoption of publicly administered insurance may help contain short-term healthcare costs in contrast to fluctuating market-based plans, but long-term equity may appear far off in the distance. This seems even more true with the rising premium costs for healthcare in California and other states as I write this book.

One thing is for sure, wrote Don McCanne of Physicians for a National Health Program in 2001: "Equity is to be clearly distinguished from the unrealistic and inequitable goal of equality in healthcare. Equal access to cosmetic surgery, to penthouse suites in ivory tower medical centers, or to detrimental high-technology interventions would waste resources and introduce inequity by forcing some to pay for such excessive services that are utilized by others. That would be unfair."

Community health centers and psychiatric facilities are going to have different definitions of legitimacy and fairness in resource allocation than crowded general hospitals. Child-based practices uphold their own definitions too.

Dr. Zarr, who was introduced in Chapter 1, practices at Unity Healthcare, which epitomizes the concept of equity in healthcare through its open-door policy for a patient base that includes 82,000 patients and up to 530,000 routine visits annually. Unity's mission is to offer a continuum of medical care and human services to uninsured, underserved, and poor residents of the District of Columbia. It's currently the largest primary healthcare agency in the area, with a team of more than 850 compassionate, multicultural professionals that include medical providers, nurses, medical and dental assistants, pharmacists, counselors, and social workers.

Further, as stated on Unity's website, "Unity has a network of 29 health centers and a mobile medical outreach vehicle, which are strategically located within all eight wards of our city. In addition, we offer a full-range of primary healthcare services that reach every facet of our community to include, but not limited to, the homeless, working poor, under/uninsured, infants, school-age children, the elderly, persons living with HIV/AIDS and/or hepatitis, as well as those who are incarcerated and recently released from jail and prisons."

The reason for describing a network like Unity in detail is simple: its patient population makes up the very base that some high-income citizens argue should not receive care in the same system that they contribute to. Their idea of equity as shown in the heated televised healthcare debates revolves around income level, sense of entitlement through being an American citizen, and the list goes on.

Equity is most definitely the aim that carries emotion and requires soft-skill approaches to, once defining it, achieving it. Aspects fall into Chapter 3, on care ethics.

Finally, the six aims that are necessary for a comprehensive quality transformation are followed by a list of principles that support them:

- Organizational culture
- Leadership driven
- All levels of staff involved
- Medical staff must be engaged
- Outcomes aligned with incentives
- Accountability
- Right quality structure
- Inter- and intradepartmental partnerships

This list is relatively complementary to the criteria as established within the National Institute of Standards and Technology (NIST) (an agency of the U.S. Department of Commerce) Malcolm Baldrige National Performance Excellence Program criteria.

- Healthcare and processes
- Customers
- Workforce
- Leadership and governance
- Finance and markets

Addressing the principles above, both holistically and at the most tactical of levels within your organization, should promote greater effectiveness and efficiency across the criteria mentioned above. Becoming more and more popular among healthcare institutions, these criteria have allowed many organizations to develop a standard, and institutionalize quality requirements and improvement programs to empower teams and healthcare professionals in improving patient care while amplifying the overall capability and efficiency of the organization.

In the 2011 Baldrige review, the Henry Ford Health System (HFHS) in Michigan was one of the few winners of the Malcolm Baldrige National Quality Award, demonstrating its achievements in quality improvement over many years of rigorous application of improvement methods and holistic quality improvement programs for patients, the organization, and its employees. Awarded by the Office of the President of the United States, and subsequently the Secretary of Commerce, HFHS was recognized for its reduction in unintended patient hazards, while establishing a zero-defect, no-excuses approach to patient services. One of its prized innovations is what it refers to as the Perfect Depression Program—an evidence-based, integrated method that brings together multiple services, from home health services to pharmaceutical services to optometry care, to increase brand recognition and access to new customers. The results of implementation of such a quality system are certainly there—from the Michigan-based Bronson Methodist Hospital's reduction of its mortality rate from 4.8 percent in 2002 to 3.5 percent in 2005, to its reduction in staff turnover from 5.6 percent to 4.7 percent. There are plenty of examples of amplified performance improvement in the face of adversity and an austere healthcare environment, and the implementation of a viable, credible quality program was the key to success for many. But, it was following a standard method and implementing it thoroughly to promote organizational success while minimizing residual challenges. Addressing numerous key areas of the organization is vital to Baldrige's holistic approach (Figure 2.2):

1. Leadership
2. Strategic planning

3. Customer focus
4. Measurement, analysis, and knowledge management
5. Workforce focus
6. Operations focus
7. Results

These areas also outline the criteria needed for an organization to address as part of its Baldrige journey. With the criteria available for a very small fee, the return is clearly substantial, but requires organizational adoption.

In the American Hospital Association's annual survey of hospitals in the United States during 2008, there were a total of 5,815 registered hospitals, 5,010 community hospitals, 213 federal government hospitals, and 447 nonfederal psychiatric hospitals. Also, the total admissions in all U.S. registered hospitals was 37,529,270.

From Baldrige Performance Excellence Program, *2013, 2013–2014 Healthcare Criteria for Performance Excellence* (Gaithersburg, MD: U.S. Department of Commerce, National Institute of Standards and Technology, http//www.nist.gov/baldrige/publications/hc_criteria.cfm).

Figure 2.2   Malcolm Baldrige quality improvement framework.

Given the enormity of a year's worth of care generated through the system, is there a threshold for installing a baseline of standards and a level of quality that we can all depend on?

"I do believe there is a threshold that can be created in terms of minimum substandards that all hospitals would have to meet in order to achieve a certain level of quality," said Kathy Chavanu Gorman, MSN, RN, chief operating officer at Children's National Medical Center in Washington, D.C.

"There must be like populations. In healthcare, we have so many variables that we're compared to highly regulated industries such as the airlines industry to ensuring safety and ongoing care. They have one set of processes, one overall mission. Does that mean we cannot improve care? Absolutely not."

Formerly the senior vice president and chief nursing officer at Children's Hospital of Philadelphia, Gorman has also held positions at the Hospital for Sick Children in Washington, D.C., and St. Joseph Hospital at Creighton University in Omaha. This diversity in healthcare settings alone has given Gorman the experience needed to profess solutions from a holistic vantage point.

She added: "There is a set of core metrics that can be established systems-wide. They would have to be apples-to-apples hospitals. You can't expect a critical care 20-bed hospital in rural Nebraska to compete against an academic 500- or 600-bed hospital in an urban care setting. We can look at our commonalities; for example, we all have to provide immediate stabilization and treatment for patients. Also, patient safety is paramount; checking the ID band, writing down and reading back when a physician calls an order, washing our hands before every patient encounter. This gets into mandatory reporting. It's a challenge, but we have to get there."

Keeping a patient safe, reporting data, cutting the cost of surgical equipment, and shortening a patient's wait time in the emergency room are each full-time initiatives at times.

The theory of constraints can apply to all of these common tasks through five steps, which enjoin and naturally provide that threshold that Gorman refers to. Once you consider each of the steps, you'll note the inherent logic in this body of knowledge handed down to countless process improvement specialists. Thought of as a whole, the team effort alone consists of not only the creation of solutions, but also the level of communication and collaboration that success shows off.

The five steps of the theory of constraints in greater detail are (Figure 2.3)

1. Identify the constraint (the resource or policy that prevents the organization from obtaining more of the goal). In healthcare settings, physical constraints would be the number of examination rooms, physicians, nurses, and clerks. Policy constraints would be ineffective policies,

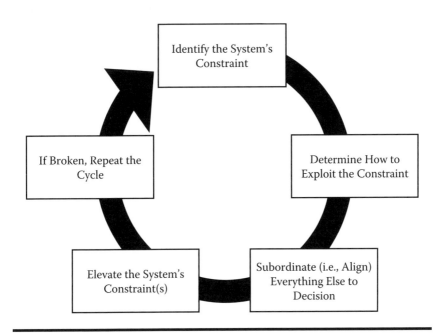

Figure 2.3 Theory of constraints cyclical framework.

measures, or behavior patterns. Is the support staff large enough for each physician and number of patients? This is one of the most common concerns today.

2. Decide how to exploit the constraint (get the most capacity out of the constrained process). If the constraint is physical, the objective is to make the constraint remarkably effective. Again, is the use of support staff, supplies, equipment, budgets, and rooms being maximized toward the goal of caring for the individual patient?

3. Subordinate all other processes to the above decision (align the whole system or organization to support the decision made above). Every step of the process needs to coincide with an overarching strategy for greatness.

4. Elevate the constraint (make other major changes needed to break the constraint). This step requires a financial or time investment (staff or space expansion, for example).

5. If, as a result of these steps, the constraint has moved, return to step 1; don't let inertia become the constraint.

   In other words, process improvement is an ongoing journey.

Thinking back to the idea of developing standards equitable to all, what would you say if I told you comparing the performance and capability of a hospital could be done against the war-fighting effectiveness of an aircraft carrier?

Prepare yourself. To this day, decisions are made on some of the nation's most expensive, elaborate, and complicated programs by what is often referred to as a BOGSAT (bunch of guys sitting around a table). I am not talking about hundreds of thousands of dollars, or even millions. *Hundreds of billions.* So, while the acronym makes most in the military snicker at its utterance, I imagine you're not laughing.

"Captain, my program is failing!" These are the screams of numerous military service men and women begging for the ongoing saturation of their programs with taxpayer dollars. Of course, this ultimately ends up as an ineffective and inefficient means for managing, and subsequently reporting the status of, those programs. Clearly, there is a problem for developing and *requiring* a system or process for the construction of applicable and equitable metrics to amplify the understanding by program managers and leaders of critical assets that are intended to protect this country.

The development and institutionalization of standardized metrics and a means for reporting progress is not contained to the Navy. But, the solutions can be similar, and it starts with one word: *meaningful.* As a decision maker, you and others make challenging decisions on topics that are generally too complex for the mind to accurately simplify. The economic environment is austere. The healthcare industry is certainly austere—just think of how many organizations, patients, providers, businesses, and others will be impacted by the implementation of the Affordable Care Act (ACA). Regardless, one concept should always drive your decisions—*meaningful* data and information as derived from depth and broadness of your devotion to analysis.

But, how do you know when enough is enough? If you can go to bed at night saying that you're comfortable with the decision you made because you made it with meaningful data and information driven by an equitable means for analyzing options, then I imagine you've made a more informed—and likely better—decision. However, getting others to support your efforts in installing such analysis and reporting requirements is truly the crux to achieving success.

I'm by no means a salesman, but I also don't need to be. Neither do you. OK, you're at a point where you are willing to accept this notion of equitability and analysis in your endeavors to improve healthcare, whether you're a hospital CEO, nurse manager, Secretary of the Department of Health and Human Services, or a provider seeking some way to tell what's really going on in your emergency room. Now, you need to convince—not sell—your newfound notion to others.

If I were to tell you that I was the president of the United States and you had never heard of me and Barack Obama is currently residing in the White House, what would be your reaction? I imagine you would respond with, "Sure, buddy. And, I'm the vice president. Prove it."

That's it! Prove it! We should be making decisions based on what I like to call *impact analysis*—the results of your analytical breadth and depth that subsequently provide you with better, more accurate, and quality decision-making criteria that you never had before. This means you have to think! And, simply beyond "that seems like a good decision." Develop and institutionalize your meaningful and equitable metrics (at least for a trial run for a single decision you have to make), test your theories with good data and analysis as aligned to your metrics, and present this information to others in a format they can understand. See, there's no need to sell it. There's no need to quickly search for responses to inquiring minds when you're in front of many others trying to explain why your decision makes sense. The information is right there—just get up and do something.

Six Sigma

Six Sigma has been made a star business application in various companies worldwide since its inception by Motorola in 1981. You would be hard-pressed to flip open a business management guide today and not find it listed in the index, in fact. The reason for this is simple: Six Sigma methods are created to eliminate errors and minimize variability with people across the organization whose sole focus is working on improvement. These people are considered Master Black Belts, Black Belts, Green Belts, Yellow Belts, and so on, after earning certification. For those of you statisticians, mathematicians, and traditionalists that cringe at the very thought of Six Sigma, don't fear. We all know that Six Sigma is the effective and efficient application of statistical—and other analytically charged methods—in the quest for quality improvement. Now, each Six Sigma project does involve financial goals alongside many other targets that the practice stems from.

Defined, Six Sigma derives from a statistical term that sums up your quality having <3.4 defects per million for a given product or process specification. Six levels of performance are documented. In its more modern application in various companies, Six Sigma is a methodology for reducing the variability of processes for a greater quality consistency and performance excellence. Stability, innovation, long-term vision, creativity, and rationality are all inherent objectives.

In a manufacturing setting, customer satisfaction in quality, cost, and delivery is the first priority of business. In a health-care setting, replace the word *customer* with *patient* and there you have your reason for even implementing the strategy in the first place. Value stream mapping, or understanding your business processes, is performed to identify problematic areas where wastes, or non-value-adding costs, are eating away at your system. Decisions can be made based on the data and facts collected from the value stream mapping.

The waste observed in day-to-day efforts alone will often surprise leadership into ordering an entire redesign of a department or restructuring an organization, beginning the road to sustainable improvement. Once performance is measured without the waste that once existed, individuals and teams can learn a better way of doing the job.

As of 2006, Motorola reported more than $17 billion in savings from devoting time to Six Sigma projects, so why wouldn't other companies want to follow this example? The simple answer is *change*.

A change in strategy, planning, human capital management, process control, and sometimes even location is crucial to the success of a Six Sigma project. Studies have shown that the majority of human beings have a hard time adjusting to the most basic changes in their day—whether it's their driving route to work because of a detour or the time they eat lunch because of an impromptu meeting called by a coworker. Therefore, as you can imagine, there are many challenges a hospital or critical care unit could face when bringing about change in processes and services. Still, most facilities cannot afford to opt for the option of *not* implementing the change.

The most common factors involved with successful Six Sigma projects in healthcare organizations include the following:

1. Establishing full physician and staff support and effective communication
2. Identifying problem areas from patient surveys, complaints, and equipment failures
3. Brainstorming and selecting the most beneficial, cost-effective achievable project
4. Establishing teams with various backgrounds in order to promote creativity
5. Training physicians and staff in quality principles
6. Establishing clear goals and requirements (i.e., return on investment (ROI))
7. Delegating responsibilities and stressing accountability
8. Identifying the proper quality of Six Sigma techniques and tools to use
9. Setting objectives and metrics in order to track, measure, and analyze data
10. Rewarding successes and achievements

Of course none of these factors are far-flung from what hospitals should exist for in the first place, but the strategies all require money, time, and personnel to implement. Senior leaders must be the unwavering champions. In general, this means that they must ensure training of employees is carried out to the full extent by paid consultants, new software or web-based tools are installed, coursework is completed, and facilities are prepared with a conducive infrastructure for the changes that will take place. Collaboration at all levels is imperative and data must drive the process.

As a note to the cost of implementing a Six Sigma initiative, it's more common for decision makers to talk about the cost associated with the errors that existed before the techniques and training were implemented than the bill they accrued in hiring a process improvement consultant, training their staff, and installing the proper project management software, for instance.

In April 2013, I read a letter from the CEO of a hospital in Washington, D.C., utterly begging his employees to find ways to make things better. Although I believe wholeheartedly in providing some empowerment to provide insights from those that are constantly working day to day with the same deficiency-plagued systems and processes, it's not enough. The message—I felt—made me feel as if they were hurting so bad that it was a cry for help, and leadership either didn't know what to do or didn't want to spearhead improvement initiatives. Perhaps my email to this CEO later in the day made him think about the need to do more than this, or just made him mad. Nevertheless, I didn't get a response.

It's already been stated that leaders must champion improvement efforts. But two things that are absolutely critical, especially in the environment today, in achieving success are

1. Take a risk, for goodness sake. Too scared to spend money on a Six Sigma effort, or too worried that the return will not be enough to justify the spending in the first place. Or, just too scared to see what's on the other side that you've been ignoring—or simply unaware of—for so long. First, of course there will be improvement initiatives that require an investment, and perhaps some will not give you the immediate return you had hoped for. But, did you consider the impact—the future operational,

behavioral (yes, people are excited for making their jobs easier and better while not losing the quality of patient services!), and managerial impacts of pushing forward? Don't be scared of what's on the other side or worried about how the hospital might look in realizing you're not as good as you had always claimed with a "leap frog," Joint Commission, or some other accreditation or recognition. Shoot, even being International Organization for Standardization (ISO) certified means you can have the most ineffective and inefficient standards and processes in place without even knowing it. Just take a little risk and see what's on the other side.

2. To take a risk, following the same old Six Sigma methods may or may not work for you. I don't believe in letting prepackaged "tools" drive my analysis or improvement efforts, but rather in letting my *creativity* drive a means for improving systems and processes regardless of industry or challenge. And, I would expect the same for you. But, how do we do this? Daniel Pink, author of several best-selling books, including *A Whole New Mind*, recently provided me with his thoughts on being creative. "There is no simple recipe. But the ingredients are pretty straightforward." Here is a list of those ingredients according to Mr. Pink:

   a. Being curious
   b. Having the autonomy to direct one's own work
   c. Reading, listening, and watching a variety of topics, disciplines, and industry
   d. Surrounding yourself with people who are diverse in outlook but who share your curiosity, autonomy, and multiness

Granted, a recipe can be tweaked ever so slightly and still produce the same—or similar—end state. But, you still have to put forth the effort to effect change, not to mention taking a little risk and being creative in the process.

Six Sigma Cost Breakdown

In a July 2008 article on quality for the *MBA Journal*, quality analyst Tony Jacowski wrote, "Poor quality leads to higher costs as well as customer dissatisfaction. The sales that are lost means loss of revenue, which may become critical if not handled carefully and on time. Thorough measurement of quality can help prevent such situations. The biggest amount of loss is from non-conformance detected by customers. Along with the cost of repair or replacement, companies lose out on goodwill and reputation, which worsens when the customer informs other customers about the same. Further costs may have to be incurred if there is any litigation. Additionally, if the detection of errors is done in the early stages when they happen, the causes can be determined easily. A time lag in detection leads to further delay in removal, unless the exact reason is located."

If a company plans for a 100-hour course (40 hours of classroom instruction, 60 hours of required online assignments) for a staff member to obtain a Six Sigma Black Belt certification at approximately $3,000, significant results are possible within months of the training. Most full-time professionals attend class one night per week, so the certification takes about three months. In this short time, employees learn various and practical tools that can apply to any business setting.

Consider all the ways that the following course objectives provided by the American Society for Quality could assist a healthcare team:

■ Understand key drivers for business; understand key metrics/scorecards.
■ Use the correct formula to calculate ROI.
■ Use graphical, statistical, and qualitative tools to understand customer feedback.
■ Calculate defects per unit (DPU), rolled throughput yield (RTY), and defect per million opportunities (DPMO) sigma

levels; understand how metrics propagate upward and allocate downward; compare and contrast capability, complexity, and control; manage the use of sigma performance measures (e.g., parts per million [PPM], DPMO, DPU, RTY, cost of poor quality [COPQ]) to drive enterprise decisions.

■ Understand and present financial measures and other benefits (soft and hard) of a project.

■ Understand and use basic financial models (e.g., net present value [NPV], ROI); describe, apply, evaluate, and interpret cost of quality concepts, including quality cost categories, data collection, reporting, etc.

■ Define, select, and use (1) affinity diagrams, (2) interrelationship diagrams, (3) tree diagrams, (4) prioritization matrices, (5) matrix diagrams, (6) process decision program charts (PDPCs), and (7) activity network diagrams.

Regarding the use of an affinity diagram, this tool is very beneficial in reducing a large amount of data, or complex issues, into smaller subject matter categories from which relationships and common themes can be analyzed. The types of information that match the affinity diagram best are patient complaints, suggestions, long patient or employee surveys, and brainstorming session ideas.

A favorite exercise in the classroom by Six Sigma instructors is to create some variation of an affinity diagram with the following steps: Introduce the issue that needs to be discussed in a loose, generally vague way to leave room for *all* discussion points. Capture ideas by writing them on Post-it notes. When the Post-it notes fill up an 8 × 11-inch sheet of paper, start another, keeping them all in a notebook. Organize the ideas into subcategories, titling each with a logical heading. Place all the remaining ideas that don't align with the subcategories to the side, which naturally leads to the process of elimination (Figure 2.4). Some ideas will not be as relevant as others and may be part of another conversation or brainstorm that needs to happen at a later time.

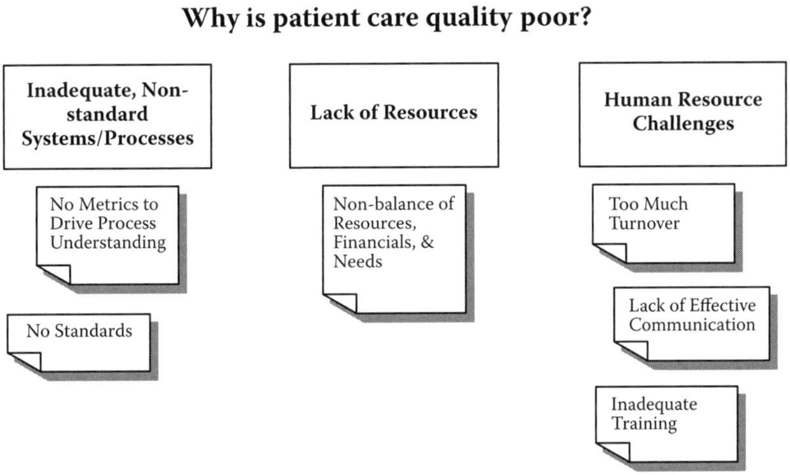

Why is patient care quality poor?

Figure 2.4   Assessing patient care quality using an affinity diagram.

With these basic steps, you've just embarked on a miniature but mighty Six Sigma management and planning tool.
Now, either using this baseline to lead into the use of another
method or tool or modifying it to fit the problem you face will
allow you to address various challenges with some innovation,
allowing the tools to augment leadership-sponsored teamwork
and performance improvement.

Picture of Six Sigma Health

It would be impossible to discuss all of Valley Baptist Health
System's achievements in 2007, the same year that marked
the U.S. economic downturn that then resulted in millions of
people losing either all of their health insurance or at least a
good dose of it. In this climate of discontent, Valley Baptist in
South Texas reigned in process improvement, earning many
firsts and setting an example of true excellence in the U.S.
healthcare industry.

Valley Baptist, which received the prestigious Malcolm Baldrige National Quality Award in 2006, reports the following strides in its organization-wide application of Six Sigma:

- Completion of Six Sigma training by 340 employees
- Design of its own Six Sigma conference, "Achieving Excellence in Healthcare through Six Sigma"
- More than 100 ongoing Six Sigma initiatives
- Global Six Sigma Platinum Award for Most Outstanding Organizational Achievement through Six Sigma
- Global Six Sigma Best Achievement of Six Sigma in Healthcare
- Number 1 ranking in nation for heart failure by Centers for Medicaid and Medicare Services
- Texas Healthcare Excellence Award for Management of Heart Failure and Heart Attack; Quality Improvement Award for Surgical Care Improvement Project Core Measures

Speaking on being the pillar of Six Sigma strength, himself a certified Master Black Belt, Dr. Tomas Gonzalez, senior vice president and chief quality officer for Valley Baptist Health System, told *Quality Digest* in a May 2008 interview with Mike Richman, "Key caregivers and staff are involved from the beginning of each Six Sigma project, because Six Sigma initiatives require the input and participation of those closest to the care or procedure. Patients, family members, physicians, and other customers provide input through the voice of the customer, the starting point for any Six Sigma initiative. Nurses, physicians, pharmacists, suppliers, and others who are closest to the process provide input through four-hour Six Sigma workouts, designed to quickly elicit effective, doable improvement ideas, and to develop a who, what, when, and why (4W) plan for implementing change.

"For the more-extensive initiatives, physicians, pharmacists, nurses, respiratory therapists, and other frontline staff serve on the initiative team, under the leadership of a Six Sigma Green Belt and Master Black Belt. Frontline caregivers are involved in developing the multifaceted improvement efforts; the process control plans and control methods; determining ways to engrain accountability for the standard operating procedures for individual nurses and staff; and calculating the effect on patient care."

Again, this is a renowned physician speaking about a program that's traditionally been lauded in Fortune 500 companies and manufacturing environments. Gonzalez's tone is one of mature dedication and confidence around this subject matter. This is just to say that every level of healthcare worker can be a champion of quality and improvement in their daily commitment to patient care.

So, what did Valley Baptist improve upon and how did this 800-bed hospital enlist Six Sigma with such passion?

First, it didn't begin alone. General Electric Healthcare's Performance

Solutions group joined and shared its own learnings for the first two years, according to a case study on HealthExecutive. com. Valley Baptist's key challenges included admitting and discharge processes, operating rooms and emergency departments, and laboratories. Over the course of their teamwork, comprehensive management and leadership systems were put into place, such as a year-round operating calendar and structured human resources processes.

More recently, Valley Baptist's heart management program has been the token case study in many publications and conferences for its number 1 ranking in the nation by a pay-for-performance project conducted by the federal government. It's no surprise that the hospital credits Six Sigma for this praise, with two initiatives being the focal point for success. The initiatives centered on evidence-based medical management of heart failure and acute myocardial infarction patients, resulting in lower death rates, lower readmission rates, and shorter lengths of stay in the hospital.

Heart management. Six Sigma. Sounds like a fish riding a bicycle. How did the two intersect? Gonzalez detailed the phases in *Quality Digest*:

> During the "define" phase of the initiative, the focus was placed on improved compliance with national core measures for treatment of heart failure patients. Two "Green Belts in training," the nurse manager of cardiac rehab for Valley Baptist, the ED nurse manager, cardiologists, family practitioners, cardiac ED physicians, medical-surgical staff, cardiac rehab, CHF clinic and ED nurses, pharmacists, case managers, and documentation specialists all participated in the initiative.
>
> During the "measure" phase, Valley Baptist staff reviewed 300 medical records and created an aggregate score for each measure. The baseline data review showed a sigma score of 1.7, or a 58-percent yield, for complying with heart failure core measures and a defect per million opportunities (DPMO) of 420,000.
>
> During the "analyze" phase, the team employed analysis tools to identify the greatest variances in the process, and used brainstorming to assess barriers to uniformity and to identify ideas for improvement. Ideas included staff and physician education, a process to identify heart failure patients on admission, and documentation tools and reminders to facilitate compliance. Physicians on Valley Baptist's cardiac care committee were made aware of the importance of their involvement. The team then developed a new standard procedure to address heart failure patients.
>
> Lastly, the initiative reached 100-percent compliance with heart failure core measures in 2005, and this result has been sustained over time at the

near-perfect Six Sigma level. From October 2005 to
August 2006, the improvements affected 626 patients.
The improvements are projected to affect as many
as 7,000 patients over the next ten years in the
Harlingen branch of Valley Baptist alone.

Processes are measured long before any solution is implemented, to obtain the baseline statistics on how often a standard is being met under the current procedures. Solutions
are tried and retooled in the pilot phase. Once success is
achieved, the improvements are applied on a larger scale in
the control phase, and eventually rolled out throughout the
hospital and health system. Solutions and ideas for improvement are rewarded, but an even greater emphasis is placed on
day-to-day execution of the improved procedures to ensure
continuous success. Decision support tools are employed
continuously, including electronic spread sheets which divide,
measure, and analyze every step in the process in great
detail. This helps in eliminating or consolidating unnecessary steps until only truly value-added steps are left in the
process. An example of how a project is initiated involves
our Six Sigma initiative on heart failure management. During
the "define" phase of the initiative, the focus was placed on
improved compliance with national core measures for treatment of heart failure patients. A team of two "Green Belts
in Training," the nurse manager of cardiac rehab for Valley
Baptist and the ED [emergency department] nurse manager,
along with cardiologists, family practitioners, cardiac ED physicians, medical-surgical staff, cardiac rehab, CHF clinic and
ED nurses, pharmacists, case managers, and documentation
specialists tackled this clinically critical initiative. During the
"measure" phase of the project, Valley Baptist staff reviewed
300 medical records and created an aggregate score for each
measure. The baseline data review showed a sigma score
of 1.7 or a 58-percent yield for complying with heart failure
core measures and a defect per million opportunities (DPMO)

of 420,000. During the "analyze" phase, the team employed Six Sigma analysis tools to identify the greatest variances in the process, and used brainstorming to assess barriers to uniformity and to identify ideas for improvement. Ideas included staff and physician education, a process to identify heart failure patients on admission, and documentation tools and reminders to facilitate compliance. Physicians on Valley Baptist's cardiac care committee were made aware of the importance of their involvement. The team then developed a new standard procedure to address heart failure patients. The initiative reached 100-percent compliance with heart failure core measures in 2005, and this result has been sustained over time at the near-perfect six sigma level. From October 2005 to August 2006, the improvements affected 626 patients. The improvements are projected to affect as many as 7,000 patients over the next ten years in Harlingen alone.

Define, Measure, Analyze, Improve, Control

O'Quinn suggests using the structured approach of DMAIC: define, measure, analyze, improve, and control. Compared to other improvement methodologies, DMAIC's five phases more explicitly convey the steps required for process improvement. DMAIC is a methodology, and the tools and techniques vary depending on the situation. What is often said about DMAIC is that the technique does require rigorous data collection, measurements, and analysis so that a problem can be clearly identified and the proper solution can be implemented and controlled.

O'Quinn emphasized that primary focus on patient satisfaction is the bridge to all of the steps involved in DMAIC. His own daily experience rooted in this methodology is no surprise, considering the type of healthcare setting he works for.

The DMAIC framework provides you with a starting point from which to systematically navigate a particular challenge, with a focus on an end state of greater effectiveness and efficiency. Although a relatively simple concept that allows you to infuse your own creativeness in approaching a particular problem, following a structured process is key to—at a very minimum—gaining experience and insight into improving processes.

Carilion Clinic, comprised of more than 600 physicians in a multispecialty group practice and 8 not-for-profit hospitals, follows the business approach of lean Six Sigma in all of its specialty areas. Each worker is trained to focus on consistently practicing accepted standards of care and recognizing when efficiency can be improved.

The clinic has acquired many awards for excellence in everything from electronic record management, supply chain leadership, superior workforce training, patient safety, and quality to bariatrics, home care, and orthopedic care.

Carilion Clinic's own goals of performance improvement incorporate some of the principles discussed in this book, including care equity, innovation, family-centered care, and safety: Provide reliable healthcare services to all who could benefit based upon scientific knowledge. Refrain from providing unnecessary and costly services to those not likely to benefit. Avoid waste, wait times, and harmful delays. Provide care that does not vary because of personal characteristics (gender, ethnicity, geographic location, and socioeconomic status). Effectively manage Carilion Clinic's resources to ensure the best possible care is delivered to the maximum number of patients.

O'Quinn defined the following steps of DMAIC (Figure 2.5) as having equal importance:

■ *Define.* Clarify the purpose and scope of the project. Compile a charter of information gleaned from four questions: What is your objective? What is the timeline for completion? What is your budget for the initiative? Who are the team members?

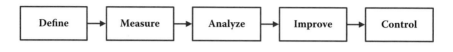

Figure 2.5 Six Sigma DMAIC problem-solving framework.

- *Measure.* Identify crucial measures and gather baseline data. After all, improvements must be verified against the "existing state" in order to create the "ideal state."
- *Analyze.* Determine the root cause of issues and inefficiencies (or waste). Confirm any relationships between the causes and the existing performance or results.
- *Improve.* Begin to meet the project's goal(s) by countering the root cause(s) documented in the analyze phase. Confirm the improvements by techniques such as brainstorming and piloting improvement programs.
- *Control.* Set up ongoing tracking methods and a plan for correction should the same issues or new obstacles arise. At this point, the results should be shared with everyone within the organization, including stakeholders.

"For some projects, the tools and techniques may be as simple as a tally sheet, a Pareto chart, and a cause-and-effect diagram," O'Quinn explains. "Complex projects may require the more complex tools and techniques of Six Sigma, such as logistic regression, analysis of variance, and design of experiments (DOE)."

According to iSixSigma.com, logistics regression is a framework for measurement and prediction that assesses the relationship between two variables. The variables are typically detailed in table form to review customer complaints before a plot, or chart for action, is created. This method is most successful when the project manager is skilled in statistics and high-level business intelligence.

"DMAIC is a methodology that works regardless of the complexity of the tools and techniques applied. Without a methodology, improvement initiatives will likely continue down the path of inefficiency and ineffectiveness."

I agree. However, I am quite the fan—as you already know from previous sections—that simply relying on the same methods and "tools" doesn't always produce the results you seek. Thus, I challenge you to not only follow a systematic method for addressing needed change in your organization, but also do it with an open mind, and some creativity. There should be a "one size *does not always* fit all" attitude when spearheading improvement engagements, but these tools and methods certainly provide a great starting point to keep you on the right path.

QD: What's your personal vision for improvement at Valley Baptist?

TG: For our organization as a whole, my vision is for Valley Baptist to be an international leader in promoting quality healthcare and in teaching other health-care institutions how to achieve success through Six Sigma and other quality improvement tools. We have already taken the first steps in this leadership role by holding our own conference, where we showed more than 130 people how Six Sigma can be successfully applied to healthcare.

We have been contacted by other organizations interested in having us present this methodology on-site to their personnel—both in the United States and Mexico—and we have been invited to speak at quality improvement conferences and gatherings literally across the globe, from London to Harvard. I see what we started here at Valley Baptist—deep in South Texas—as having national implications. Health-care administrators, quality managers, office managers, physicians, and nurses can learn creative new strategies that will allow them to enhance quality of care, transform business processes, and maximize savings, which would go a long way in helping our country to meet the challenges it faces in healthcare today and into the future. My vision is that we will continually improve to the point that every patient will know that every time they are admitted to the hospital we will do everything possible, according to evidence-based medicine, every time, to deliver the best possible care.

QD: What's next for Valley Baptist? Have you considered applying for the Malcolm Baldrige National Quality Award?

TG: Yes, we are working on applying for the Baldrige Award. In addition, we have another wave of initiatives underway at both hospitals, and we are refocusing our quality initiatives department to achieve greater participation and input from nurses, physicians, and board members in selecting and implementing our quality improvement initiatives. We will seek to continually raise the bar as we strive to deliver the highest quality of care to each and every patient and to be at the very top of the nation when it comes to delivering quality healthcare.

Our efforts at quality improvement were recently recognized when Valley Baptist, Harlingen, was named one of the Thomson top 100 hospitals in the nation for cardiovascular care. In addition, Valley Baptist, Brownsville, has been recognized by the Alliance for Cardiac Care Excellence for making significant improvements in cardiac care. More than 95 percent of the patients at Valley Baptist, Brownsville, received care according to 12 quality measures in 2006. This national recognition is from a coalition which includes the American College of Cardiology, the Centers for Medicare and Medicaid Services, the American Health Quality Association and the American Heart Association.

Design of Experiments

Design of experiments (DOE) has been used extensively by DuPont, Dow, BF Goodrich, and others for over 30 years. DOE was introduced by Genichi Taguchi in Japan in the early sixties with the pursuit of reducing time to market in product development, improving research and development programs, developing better products faster, and easing technology transfer in manufacturing environments.

A leader in a combination of skills rarely paired together—textile engineering (kimonos) and statistics—Taguchi received the Indigo Ribbon from the emperor of Japan in 1986 for his outstanding contributions to Japanese economics and industry. That year, he also received the International Technology Institute's Willard F. Rockwell Medal for combining engineering and statistical methods to achieve rapid improvements in cost and quality by optimizing product design and manufacturing processes.

In healthcare, DOE holds the most promise in improving patient safety, reducing costs in areas such as emergency wait times, and selecting the proper treatment in operating rooms to result in fast patient recovery times. Outcome governs the method, not ideas or assumptions.

According to the Quality Portal, DOE is a series of structured tests designed in which planned changes are made to the input variables of a process or system. The effects of these changes on a predefined output are then assessed. The method allows a judgment on the significance to the output of input variables acting alone, as well as input variables acting in combination with one another. The order of tasks to using this tool starts with identifying the input variables and the response (output) that is to be measured.

For each input variable, a number of levels are defined that represent the range for which the effect of that variable is desired to be known. An experimental plan is produced that tells the experimenter where to set each test parameter for each run of the test. The response is then measured for each run. The method of analysis is to look for differences between response (output) readings for different groups of the input changes. These differences are then attributed to the input variables acting alone (called a single effect) or in combination with another input variable (called an interaction).

Because DOE is team oriented, project members should come from a variety of backgrounds in order to create a rich initiative. The tool is used to answer specific questions. In order to draw the maximum amount of information, a full matrix is needed that contains all possible combinations of factors and levels.

If its principles sound highly mathematical, DOE's emphasis on numbers is essential to Taguchi's statistical theory to improve the mean outcome of a process.

You've Paid for the Consultant, Now What?

Many hospitals now have a "responsibility tree" that typically includes the hospital board of directors, a quality and safety council, a crisis reduction committee, and a clinical effectiveness committee or some variation of such. Again, these projects require a great deal of attention, support, and resources at all levels of the organization. Every level of worker will bring specific contributions, and every level of qualifications must enter the circle in order for it to be completely functional.

The outside consultant who oversees the implementation is trained to both respect the relationships within the organization and quietly overlook them, so each team member is treated the same for the sanity of the project. This is like any project that involves a huge chunk of time and multiple resources, but this maturity is highly imperative in healthcare settings because the team has to also account for the silent partner and biggest beneficiary, the patient. In other words, the consultant's time cannot be spent dealing with the water cooler office drama that sometimes comes with overworked, underpaid coworkers.

Do you know the price of a consultant? Have you ever considered a consultant? Would you contractually demand a positive return on your investment or go in expecting change and fluffy bunnies because you paid for a top-tier firm? I'm definitely not here to tell you how to hire, manage, and fire consultants, but rather to make sure that you stay involved with a consultant on hand. I have seen far too many improvement efforts fail simply because leaders were not involved. They expected everything to come from the consultant. The consultant is not the face to all staff. The consultant does not drive the continuous adherence to policies and procedures, nor does he or she front the resources required to execute the effort.

Let's look at an example. One of the most obvious tools a responsibility tree can use to implement a Six Sigma program is W. Edwards Deming's plan-do-check-act (PDCA) cycle:

- *Plan.* Form a hypothesis and create an experimental design.
- *Do.* Test the hypothesis.
- *Check.* Verify the replicability of the experiment.
- *Act.* Make this proven hypothesis a part of the standard.

Many of you reading this may already be familiar with this method, but for those that aren't, what would the implementation of this actually look like?

Aligning each team member's responsibilities to each phase of the PDCA cycle is important to setting expectations early, allowing everyone to understand where they're going and why. However, it's not enough to do this only for your team members, but also for those that are recipients of care. Involving your patients in every step of your improvement efforts will actually result in that—*improvement.* Patients—or customers—aren't shy in expressing their feelings concerning their treatment, bedside manner, long waits staring at reruns of the *Cosby Show* on the waiting room television, or even the billing and other paperwork processes that they experience on each dreaded visit to the hospital. Listen to them, and continuously inject voice of the customer (VoC) in each phase. See, we're combining methods, and being a little creative! Granted, it's expected that while these things should be understood by that consultant you just hired, you need to understand that you can't sit on the sidelines. You must be involved.

Or, what about using the example provided earlier—the SIPOC? You saw how it can be used to identify relationships from one system or process to another. How might you leverage that same capability to develop a new process and inform a decision to *buy* a particular solution? Let's say that you are managing a department that currently uses a number of information technology (IT) solutions—a legacy system, a status reporting process, and various other systems/processes, perhaps even an electronic medical record (EMR) system that you purchased only a few months ago. Now, due to the challenging integration of these systems, you're stuck with a deficient hodgepodge of IT capabilities that do not share information effectively, require continuous training due to the constant upgrades and changes required to reach *some* level of functionality, and you're losing substantial time and money in getting this off the ground quickly and effectively, with a meaningful end state.

By understanding the current state of the entire organizational system, you will be able to map each system/process according to a structured method—in this case, the SIPOC— and can develop the relationships from one element of each system/process to the others.

But, that's not enough! You need to understand what the end state requirements must be to reduce costs and amplify patient care via these systems. Almost ignoring what you've accomplished on your mapping, now develop an understanding internally of what you really need to accomplish and what you, the organization, the physicians and staff, and the patients truly need. Based on those requirements, you can identify potential solutions that may—or may not—align to each of those requirements based on a series of metrics/measures that will allow you to develop an integrated picture of an option's potential performance, cost, schedule for implementation, risk, and overall value. Subsequently comparing those options will provide you with the data and information you need to make a more informed investment decision, without just jumping at a capability that may not make sense based on your organization's preparedness, capability, or organizational needs at that particular point in time. The result of using this method is a strong comparative analysis of potential options to solve your IT challenges discussed earlier. You have now aligned the organizational mission and objectives to particular requirements, and subsequently to options for improvement. However, most importantly, these options are supported by a very comprehensive analysis against specific metrics/measures that allow you to fully understand where you're at and what's out there for improvement (Figure 2.6).

With these types of tools, coupled with a little innovation, you can bring the best that a consultant may offer internally to your organization and achieve success via improvements you may have never thought possible. Thinking creatively about challenges, methods to achieve a particular result, and the impacts of various decisions is what makes a consultant valuable—you can obviously do the same.

Now, let's consider another fun case with the government. Although the infamous Department of Homeland Security (DHS) has recently been engulfed in media attention and a probing public due to its purchase of a gross amount of ammunition, it does other things than just carry guns. Can you believe that organizations today still use FORTRAN and quite obsolete snippets of software code in hodgepodge systems that manage the safety and security of our nation? They do, and while I can't say if DHS is one of them, I can say that

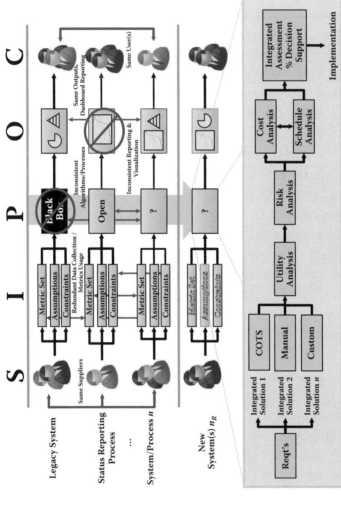

Note: n represents any integer against an infinite series. For example, if 10 systems/processes are applicable, then n = 10. n_R represents the chosen alternative based on stated functional requirements (i.e., R). "Reqt's" stands for requirements. "COTS" stands for "Commercial-Off-The-Shelf," and is considered a commercially available software or capability that may require minimal modification prior to implementation.

Figure 2.6   Expanding the role of the SIPOC model to acquisition and sustainment decision making.

it—and many other organizations—struggles with keeping team members involved in improvement efforts. For example, DHS monitors and investigates shipments in and out of the United States every second, minute, and hour of every day. With this comes a requirement for tracking systems, and with the rapid growth in complexity of software technology, it is but one of the many trying to keep up with needed improvements to ensure the safety and security of American citizens.

Let's say that DHS is faced with upgrading its technology solutions to make the monitoring of in-bound shipments more effective—meaning better screening, better binning, better processing, better inspections, and better out-processing. To evaluate numerous software options, DHS hires consultants to evaluate the current state, analyze the various potential solutions, and make recommendations for improvement. However, only two of eight required internal organizations are willing to play along. While on the surface this seems harmless, each organization's software systems are linked; i.e., they share data and information—just as healthcare reporting is intended to do. The impact of not having each team member's insight incorporated and, at a minimum, considered during the improvement effort could result in a far worse solution than is currently in place. The safety of citizens from a bioweapon, influx of contraband or weapons, or trafficking of humans is important. Just as the safety and health of a patient is important. Now, this is not meant to scare you, but to inform you of the criticality of keeping your organization involved and focused during your time of change.

Technology and People behind the Methods

Dean Athanassiades, industrial engineer and healthcare informatics expert, contributes to the field of industrial engineering, which has mastered system-oriented thinking. The field's record in better systems creation stretches into all aspects of healthcare. The Society for Health Systems, a division that offers the latest in process analytics, techniques, and methodologies for process improvement, is just one example of this effort.

Athanassiades explains: "Healthcare informatics is the unique link between what we do as industrial engineers and what IT does in healthcare. Countless implementations in healthcare have failed. By and large, this is because improving the process was ignored. If you have a flawed process, you get a bad process that runs faster. We tend to do that in healthcare IT. We have tons of bad processes. The consequence is a bigger problem. The other IE concept is that we should use systems thinking. Look at the entire system and how you want to change the entire system and then optimize—not just small pieces. It's not an easy change, but look at healthcare as a system as opposed to a bunch of independent, loosely connected things."

Athanassiades refers to the book *Redefining Healthcare* by Michael Porter and Elizabeth Olmsted Teisberg, for a kick-start in creating value for the patient rather than shifting costs and restricting services, which is often the focus of a quality-based program. Porter, a professor of business administration at the Harvard Business School, is the author of several other books on competitive analysis. Teisberg is an innovation expert. The coauthorship serves as its own example of the multidisciplined team needed to bring about profound, often overlooked strategies for improvement.

> For a service-based business, a key to success is providing a service which has value—value as defined by the consumer of the service," said O'Quinn. "Healthcare should be no different. The recipe for such a system? Combine time and competition with the seeds of culture change. One such seed is the adoption of lean principles. Those principles include defining value from the customer's perspective, then focusing on the elimination or reduction of *non-value-added* activities.

Another seed of culture change includes empowering frontline staff to improve their own processes. Depending on the process, frontline staff may include physicians, RNs, LPNs, CNAs, or housekeeping. Keep in mind empowerment isn't saying to your frontline staff, "just do it." It is first providing them with problem-solving skills and a support structure, then saying, "just do it." Healthcare organizations that move to a more consumer-driven system will have a distinct advantage in the marketplace. Much like Toyota enjoys in the automotive market.

The type of cultural transformation and openness to change that O'Quinn is referring to demands a high degree of being able to involve all team members. Open discussions and effective communication can progress by simple tasks that even elementary school teachers use to institute teams in the classroom and get to know their students: brainstorming sessions in which everyone contributes to a pool of ideas around a certain topic, icebreaker activities that support the opportunity to become comfortable with everyone and the working environment, and stories or case studies that point to real-world problems and how others solved the challenges.

Studies show that workers actually grieve the conclusion of a task, process, or routine, just as when actors who've been crammed together on stage with one another for several months and long into the night grieve when the production run of their play is over. Before starting over, workers must be encouraged to let go of the old way of communicating, a schedule, or a process.

Gorman insists that addressing three key issues facing healthcare organizations and policy makers will inevitably increase the quality of care that everyone receives.

The top issue is reimbursement. Clearly, as our unemployment rate goes up, more patients are on Medicaid.

Uncompensated care rate has increased, and we're having to provide more free care. Payers aren't paying us on time. Uncompensated care makes quality more challenging. Also, in the case of pediatrics, we don't have a set of core values or metrics that everyone is measured against. We have joint standards— Joint Commission standards—but not a scorecard or dashboard. We don't want to compare ourselves to the airline industry, but we know what they're being measured on—number of mishaps, crashes, the number of on-time arrivals, customer service issues like baggage-handling issues. They have very defined metrics. It takes organization, time and resources. Thought leaders can make a mark in modern healthcare.

Also, in people, processes and technology working together, dollars have been limited in terms of what to allocate for each of the three buckets. We have to use best practices at the provider level. Now we have a lot of data, but what are the most meaningful pieces of data that are critical to organizations and their entire systems functioning?

As discussed earlier, using only meaningful information that will drive better decisions and more effective use of systems and implementation of efficient processes is critical to success at the most tactical of healthcare operations and at the highest levels of organizational management and leadership. I can't tell you how many times I've heard the phrase "bad data in is bad data out." Personally, I'm tired of hearing it. Why would anyone institute a system that pulls in bad data? Or, why would anyone think that just having a new system is going to solve a data problem, or even the use of that data effectively? There is a plethora of data and information at our disposal, literally. And, we've already discussed potential methods for addressing these types of challenges. Ultimately, it really only takes a single, creative person to decide to do something to change the way progress and performance are assessed and reported to promote a better-run organization.

Disappointingly, I can't tell you how many systems I see to this day that claim to solve an organization's problems with a really cool voting mechanism. Keypads for all members of an organization, colocated or not, it doesn't matter. The algorithm that allows for the scoring of all votes—weighted, have you—produces amazing results. Is this the best we can do? Is a more streamlined and rapid process tied to a BOGSAT the most viable, credible, and defensible improvement we can come up with? Start with analysis and truly identify opportunities that will drive impactful, positive change through creative—and sometimes risyk—actions.

Critical Q&A

Where is the highest level of redundancy and ineffectiveness?

Diagnostic testing is the area where there is the highest level of redundancy and ineffectiveness. Different providers typically will insist that tests be redone at their institution rather than relying on high-quality tests of diagnostic capability done elsewhere. Also, many doctors will rely on their own in-office tests when they know that the quality of their equipment is less than readily available elsewhere in the community. These inefficiencies are typically driven by the desire to fully utilize expensive testing equipment and increase the return on investment on this equipment.

—Dr. James Rickert

Redundancy is not the same as ineffectiveness. In a system where harm can result from mistakes, a certain amount of redundancy is important. However, the area of communication is a set of processes that have needless redundancy, which reduces effectiveness. It is common to enter an order into the computer and then call the receiving department (a completely duplicative step). This redundancy comes from the lack of trust that healthcare workers have in their peers. Many, if not most, healthcare workers are socialized through their education experience that they and they alone are responsible. So if I am responsible, then I shouldn't trust that anyone else can do their job without me double-checking them, and we end up with communication double and triple checks. Or the ED nurse asks a patient questions, and then when the patient is admitted, the floor nurse asks the same questions.

—Charles Debusk

What tools and methods have the most significant impact on both the organization and the quality of service to the patient?

First, quality has to be a clear-cut priority at the leadership and board level. Quality must be driven by leaders. It is my feeling that there is no one tool that is the magic bullet; you need a toolbox. Lean and Six Sigma are excellent for certain process redesigns, but there are other mechanisms for instilling evidence-based guidelines. Root causes at the high-level system level, not the individual level. Using technology where you can to support quality improvement is critical. Some hospitals are constantly focused on different tools to change the culture and change behaviors from the science of improvement depending on the situation.

—Kathy Chavanu Gorman

Chapter 3

Care Ethics

"Today's debates on the public health are overwhelmed by a preoccupation with genomic advances and market innovations," Bonnie Lefkowitz wrote in her book *Community Health Centers.*

> In contrast, the early centers had a commonsense, holistic philosophy that came from understanding that good health is close to impossible if you have to choose among food, rent, and medicine.
>
> If people were hungry, health centers provided food first, then organized cooperatives and helped with employment. If sanitation was lacking, they dug privies and delivered barrels of pure water, and then campaigned for better county services. If people didn't show up, they sent buses and boats; set up shops in fields, shelters, and mobile clinics; and trained community workers in outreach and education. The centers were governed by the people who used them, and brought power where none seemed to exist.

The name Esmin Green may sound familiar, but let's pause to remember who she was and what happened to her on

June 18, 2008. Cameras panning the emergency waiting area of Kings County Hospital Center in Brooklyn were the only eyes that told the truth: Green had been waiting hours for medical attention, collapsed on the floor, went into convulsions, and died. Even then, no one ran to her side. Eventually, after more than an hour, an indifferent medic prodded Green's body with her foot, like one does to a dead insect to make sure it won't crawl and scatter again. Three minutes later, a team appeared in the area.

According to the many news accounts, Green had been admitted involuntarily to the hospital's psychiatric emergency department for agitation and psychosis. Her pastor had called 911 after witnessing Green in emotional distress because she had been hospitalized with emotional problems once before. According to the New York Civil Liberties Union, Green waited 24 hours for treatment. Records documenting Green's case beginning at admittance were falsified and seven employees were fired.

The other aspect of this tragedy is that the New York Civil Liberties Union and the Mental Hygiene Legal Service sued Kings County in federal court more than a year prior to Green's death. The groups alleged that the facility was filthy, with patients being forced to sleep in plastic chairs or on floors covered with urine, feces, and blood while waiting for beds, and that they would often go without showers, clean linens, and clean clothes. The lawsuit also claimed that patients who complained would have to face physical abuse and be injected with drugs to keep them docile.

Green was not from Texas, where, in one survey after another, the state holds the lowest ratings when it comes to the quality of healthcare residents receive. The categories, though the strongest, are not limited to care of the disabled, assistance to poor children and the malnourished, and treatment of the mentally ill.

Thousands of damning pages point to Houston's West Oaks Hospital and Arlington's Millwood Hospital, but devoting a chapter to them alone would make them a scapegoat for the 468 other facilities in the state that racked up countless complaints and the policy makers who focused on adding green space to office buildings rather than the people in need of a better way. If we break down the information to one case—one life (like Esmin Green)—we're able to call for accountability.

Language of Care

When we think of medicine as it relates to the world of science, we usually think of technical skills, mathematics, the mastery of biology, precision, and many more qualities related to hard science. On the other side of medicine, we visualize sick and grieving people and their skilled healers, nurses, and doctors. But what about soft skills? When you have the physical or mental well-being of another human being in your hands, are they just as important as sharp technical skills?

The textbook definition of soft skills includes personality traits, optimism, social graces, personal habits, friendliness, and so on. In psychiatrics, the concept is the ethics of care, and the soft-skill side of caring for a patient relates to traits valued in intimate personal relationships: sympathy, compassion, fidelity, respectfulness, and love. *Caring* specifically refers to care for, emotional commitment to, and a willingness to act on behalf of persons with whom one has a significant relationship.

Graphic depictions aren't needed in the reminder that the human relationships taking place in the ambulance, emergency room, and surgical theater involve illness, frailty, and vulnerability. Psychiatrists more readily recognize that feeling for and immersing in the other person are necessary for a moral relationship.

This is where the question of equity comes in. Should the healthcare system cultivate and nurture such relationships with all of those in need?

Noon believes that we will soon begin to resemble a national health system that may lead to a tiered system of those who can afford private care and those who can't.

"I just hope the quality and efficiency of public care is not allowed to decline. Instead, I hope the system embraces lean approaches early on with a goal of maintaining a decent level of care," Noon said.

There is a concern that decision makers across the industry echo and must continually evaluate. Again, people, procedures, and policies have become one and the same in the U.S. healthcare industry. For example, the Texas Department of State Health Services is the small hospital, but also happens to be the evening care staff, and even the medical intern, when care and professionalism take a backseat to hasty, redundant inefficiency.

The *Dallas Morning News* stated: "Texas law lets hospitals hide problems." This speaks to the issue of transparency, one that the Commonwealth Fund, a private foundation working toward healthcare process improvement, has deemed essential for three reasons: (1) to help providers improve by benchmarking their performance against others, (2) to encourage private insurers and public programs to reward quality and efficiency, and (3) to help patients make informed choices about their care.

Authors Sara R. Collins, PhD, and Karen David, PhD, expounded on this topic in the same summary for the Commonwealth Fund:

> Transparency is also important to level the playing field. The widespread practice of charging patients different prices for the same care is inherently inequitable, especially when the uninsured are charged more than other patients. But it is unreasonable to expect that information on prices, total bills (total costs to patients and insurers), and quality will cause the healthcare markets to perform like markets for other goods and services. Healthcare is not

a homogeneous commodity. Patients will never have
as much information about the care they need as the
physicians who care for them. Healthcare decisions
are often made under emergency conditions and
emotional stress. Both the insurance industry and the
healthcare delivery sector are highly concentrated,
leaving patients with few genuine choices.

But back to the case of the Texas Department of State
Health Services, one could argue that the underlying problem
is the monopoly of 15 facilities under one for-profit parent
company that has been investigated numerous times. Once the
investigations are underway, they end mysteriously with well-
paid politicians.

This is a prime reason for ushering in more specialty
"focused factories" that meet specific consumer needs, according to voices in this book. The strategy is opening the doors
to targeted competition that practices innovation, forces costs
down, and saves time, money, and resources.

In the book *Who Killed Healthcare?* author Regina
Herzlinger uses the example of Walmart, which has gone
against the concept of focused factory. As Herzlinger explains,
Walmart has squeezed vendors on pricing, product, and delivery practices; vendors comply because so much volume is
bought. In this respect, Walmart resembles the super-sized hospital, or the hungry giant that eats everything in its path. As a
result, there is no competition, no innovation, no accountability.

Returning to the aims that the Institute of Medicine has outlined, how do we tackle them and exercise care ethnics during the process? Gorman responded, "Efficiency and care can
be things like integrating the electronic medical record (EMR)
so the provider before and the provider after can be linked.
Dissolve unnecessary tests. Provide family-centered and equitable care. From a safety perspective, making sure that safety
stays in the forefront of all of our minds through technology,
processes, and the support of people to reduce errors. Push

organizations toward transparency, which does allow organizations to improve externally and internally."

Critical Q&A

Any thoughts on addressing persistent and widening disparities in care by income and race?

This problem, which is near and dear to my heart, can most effectively be addressed by lowering the high cost of healthcare. President Obama has called this "the crushing cost of healthcare." I can assure you from my own practice of medicine that these high costs reduce healthcare utilization by low-income individuals. For example, uninsured American women are more likely to die from breast cancer than are adequately insured women. Individuals make decisions based on cost that can ultimately mean the difference between life and death.

—James Rickert

I believe that the new administration will face many obstacles fighting the established medical dogma. It is too early to comment on their role on changing healthcare in our country. However, from my perspective, the new administration may have no other choice but to attack the healthcare crisis. My hope is that they are not influenced by the AMA and the big pharma as the only authority. If that happens, then we will have the same dismal outcome! We must educate the low-income and treat each race with compassion and enthusiasm. There is only one race when I treat a patient—the human race!

—Gez Agolli

Chapter 4

From the Exhibit Hall to Your Body

Washington Technology, an online think tank on government contracting, reported that the Agency for Healthcare Research and Quality began spending its $473 million in grants and contracts for projects to use IT systems to compare the effectiveness of medical treatments. Generating data about treatment outcomes and options is the main function of the agency's move to fulfill funding from President Obama's economic stimulus law. Categories for the grant awards include data infrastructure, dissemination, translation, and implementation.

This is just one ordinary example of many that propel technology to the center of healthcare industry change and modernization. These initiatives prove to add credibility to the universal call for action and attention to what some have called a "crisis," "sick system," and "flat-lined system."

The relationship between industrial engineers and technology is not one of unconditional love. More specifically, from a systems-oriented standpoint, if the technology—such as the IT systems being funded in the economic stimulus law—makes an enterprise leaner and helps workers perform their jobs in a smarter, more efficient way, the technology serves its purpose.

If the technology is being purchased strictly to check the box of spending allocated funding on something, then without proper training of the technology, it will only add to the waste that a company may have been trying to eliminate in the first place.

Of course without a medical degree or medical title, there will be an extreme gap in the knowledge needed to assess if the technology spend is value adding or wasteful in a patient care setting. Obviously, process experts are not trained to evaluate medical conditions; they are trained to provide the design, improvement, and installation of integrated systems of people, materials, information, equipment, and energy that support the *other workings* of the healthcare environment that acts as both someone's workplace and another's treatment center.

Someone at the juncture between process training and medicine is Yuehwern Yih, PhD, a professor in Purdue's School of Engineering and director of Smart Systems and Operations Laboratory. After doing manufacturing research for more than 20 years and establishing her reputation in the field, Yih became interested in healthcare when a friend died of cancer. Alongside several graduate students, one of her first projects was to help build a nutritional supply chain for HIV patients in Kenya that utilizes industrial engineering principles.

Her newest endeavor is working with Mayo Clinic to improve care for patients with chronic diseases, an increasingly important healthcare issue across the country.

"Chronic care is one of the biggest expenses healthcare is experiencing now," Yih said. "For instance, people with diabetes can't produce enough insulin. They have to be on medication for a lifetime, and they need to manage their diseases to prevent complications. They may develop other diseases and can't recover quickly because of the diabetes."

Yih reiterated her dedication to improving performance based on the limits of resources a system has (time, space, equipment, personnel, and money) and taking a holistic approach. "One of the goals is to use industrial engineering principles to design a process to help remotely monitor the patient's condition, alert nurses and physicians when the patient is off track, and intervene as needed. In managing diabetes, taking medication alone may not be sufficient, and it requires lifestyle changes. The lifestyle changes cannot be sustained without the engagement of patients and the support of their families, friends, and social circles. Depending on the patient's preference and background, we need to customize the technologies to design an effective delivery process for individual patients."

Home to many renowned industrial engineering professors who are focusing on healthcare in their research and corporate partnerships, Purdue University also boasts the Regenstrief Center for Healthcare Engineering. The center focuses on care coordination and population health with the use of electronic health records and other technology to overcome barriers to quality care and implement projects with the potential to improve care for a group of patients.

The University of Southern California's Viterbi School of Engineering, the University of Missouri's College of Engineering, and North Carolina State's Edward P. Fitts Department of Industrial Systems Engineering are just a few examples of other colleges fusing healthcare management and process-oriented training with the use of groundbreaking technology.

There will be more on education in the coming chapters. The point is that advanced technologies are being used for material modeling and prototyping health conditions in order to engage the entire healthcare system that Yih speaks of. Engineering and computer sciences have played a significant role in medicine since the arrival of contemporary technology. It's just that with the many and varied voices calling for deep healthcare improvement, technology is now such a gigantic player in the mix that must be employed in every way possible.

Engineering professors like Yih are linking arms with enterprises such as Mayo Clinic for many reasons, but the most interesting connection is that Mayo Clinic has long been praised for using manufacturing techniques to improve the patient experience. More than 55,000 doctors, scientists, students, and allied health staff work and study at three campuses, with lean thinking, Six Sigma, and value network analysis being the backbone of many publications and research profiles that have been labeled with this recognizable brand.

For highly complicated procedures such as the *transcranial magnetic stimulation* and approximately 8,000 human studies underway at any given time, Mayo Clinic operates from what it has called "an unbroken circle." Physicians, physician-researchers, and career scientists conduct observations and pledge to share findings from research that flow back into the practice to change how patients are treated. This system guarantees that all valid information is translated into a further development, which requires a lot of the general activities already discussed: benchmarking for best practices, lean and optimization of human capital, teamwork, communication, and quality.

The Mayo Clinic defines transcranial magnetic stimulation as a procedure that uses magnetic fields to stimulate nerve cells in the brain to improve symptoms of depression. The technique is usually explored when other methods have not been successful. Images of a science fiction movie pop up when considering how the procedure works: A large electromagnetic coil is placed against your scalp near your forehead. The electromagnet used in transcranial magnetic stimulation creates painless electric currents that stimulate nerve cells in the region of the brain involving mood control and depression.

Considered the least invasive of the brain stimulation techniques applied to depression, it does have risks and side effects, ranging from headaches, twitching of facial muscles, and lightheadedness to more rare side effects, such as seizures and hearing loss. Some research has shown that transcranial magnetic stimulation improved depression symptoms, and experts continue to examine the techniques, number of stimulations needed, and best sites on the brain to stimulate. The technique is also being applied to dystonia, cerebral palsy, schizophrenia, and migraines.

This is just one description of an advancement that engineering and computer sciences has created to improve prevention or facilitate treatment in the arena of healthcare. Now, multiply that by the number of research labs, medical device manufacturers, biosciences clusters, and electronic medical record (EMR) creators in the United States, and you won't possibly be able to calculate the scale of advancements at our disposal.

With astounding technology, we have less invasive surgery, tests directed by miniature cameras that see the inside view of our internal organs but cause no pain, tracking devices for our sugar intakes, robots that aid surgeons, and automated pill dispensers.

It's safe to say that we appreciate these additions to our healthcare—even when the technology is living inside of our bodies, making the combination of blood and battery power seem absolutely surreal.

However, the healthcare community has endured forceful push-back when it comes to allowing for medical data to sync with technology. Issues of privacy, inequity, and identity theft immediately spring up.

Dealing with All the Data

As Athanassiades explains, healthcare informatics is the art and science of using information technology to improve financial and clinical outcomes in healthcare.

> If you take healthcare off of there, informatics is the application of technology to improving things. For a long time, we've fallen behind in using the power

of technology to seek out answers. Healthcare by nature is a data-rich environment; the data cannot be exploited without the use of computers. We should embrace the use of information technology in being a vehicle for clinical business and financial perspectives in contrast to looking for reasons not to use it. I'm amazed at the number of people who push back on using IT. I teach graduate courses and it appalls me when students are resistant. Put bluntly, if you were trying to pick between two banks, would you use the one that handles your information only on paper?

In any industry, information sharing or the collection of data for predictive analytics dominates business operations. Information that will somehow lead to profit in the long term via a sustained product, client, or, in the healthcare business, patient is invaluable. Therefore, companies spare no expense when it comes to the process of harvesting data and relating them as information that can be used for making decisions. Although the concept is not new, today's popularity and constant reference to "big data" demonstrates the continued need for predictive capabilities against structured and unstructured data and information that can drive decision making. Software companies in particular have courted hospitals to invest in their information channels— thus the enterprise of electronic medical records.

Hyland Software, Inc. uses the following case study to sell its OnBase solution. Based on the benefits, baby boomers would be hard-pressed to argue against the logic of having medical records online. The client is Cleveland Clinic, a name that immediately invokes trust, experience, and best practices in patient care.

Customer

One of the top hospitals in the U.S., the Cleveland Clinic treats patients from across the country and around the world. With the main campus in Cleveland, Ohio, the Cleveland Clinic also has more than 60 facilities across the region and in Florida, Canada and Abu Dhabi. In 2008, the health system recorded 3.3 million patients and 50,000 hospital admissions.

Challenges

The Cleveland Clinic realized true interoperability transcends hardware and software systems. The health system wanted to reach beyond simple data exchange to collaborate and share information regardless of location or facility, vendor or machine, file type or origin. That way clinicians would have all of a patient's information at the exact moment it is needed while staying in the Epic EMR.

Journey

The Cleveland Clinic turned to the OnBase enterprise content management (ECM) software suite to integrate clinical content like EKGs, photos, paper charts, forms, insurance information and much more. From the start, the health system knew OnBase would be one of the most important systems at the Cleveland Clinic, critical to users throughout the health system because of the information it would provide clinicians.

Before implementing, the Cleveland Clinic collaborated with other large health systems using OnBase and the Epic EMR to learn their best practices. The health system learned two key lessons: centralized scanning improves quality and reduces costs, and creating a governance committee is important to establishing enterprise standards and prioritizing projects.

Solution

The Cleveland Clinic used the lessons learned from the other hospitals to bridge the gaps between its Epic EMR and the information that exists outside of it. With 22,800 users, the Cleveland Clinic has already made 1.9 million documents viewable through Epic and the number is growing fast. Now, physicians can focus their attention on making the best decisions and spending time with patients, not trying to locate paper records.

Scanned paper documents from the HIM department, EKGs, retinal eye scans, lab test results and much more are just a mouse-click away for authorized Epic users. Secure access to the global healthcare community also allows for instant referrals in general practice medicine and specialists. Is this a sales pitch from a software company? Bona fide! However, the significance behind Cleveland Clinic's gigantic footprints in so many areas of healthcare and Hybrid Software's ability to provide an information portal that matches its needs is indeed a process improvement to look up to.

We'll never know the flaws in this partnership, but consider what the absence of electronic medical records would mean: the paper documentation of 3.3 million patients. How many of these patients would actually receive the right care for their medical condition or basic needs on an annual basis at minimum?

Why have electronic medical record systems taken so long to be implemented in clinics and hospitals? Even more than 20 years after clinics and hospitals first invested in these systems to make patient care more efficient, the rate of hospital use is still very low, according to the Centers for Disease Control. Consultants like Athanassiades are frustrated with the lack of initiative.

What I have found in the strongest resistance is rarely the technology; we can trivialize it and say it's a fear of change. But it's not just that; that reason does not consider cost. An obstacle is always financial. Who will pay for it? What are the economic benefits? When we hear that it will compromise privacy, that's a consequence that they are really not thinking about the problem critically.

Anyone that has worked in healthcare knows that the only thing that is less secure than EMR is the paper record. With that paper record, there is no trail on who even looked at it! There's a fear of standardization, a fear of control of information, which is well-founded, but the lack of electronic medical record adoption is more in the outpatient setting than the hospital setting. It's a money thing. There are regulatory obstacles for hospitals; it's questionable if the EMR can provide information to independent doctors that have to work at that hospital.

Athanassiades explained that a small facility may have to spend $50,000 on EMRs, but the operational rewards are bottomless.

The Healthcare Information Management and Systems Society has encouraged innovative use in electronic health systems, and offers an annual award ceremony to recognize small businesses that excel in the use of outpatient electronic medical records. Athanassiades points out that the people who have received these awards have small businesses. These are the pioneers. For the pressing obstacle of assuring patients that the records will only be seen by those central to their care, he says that there should be more standards.

"The value is diminished if you can't share the information freely (interoperability)," he continued. "Can you imagine buying a house and discovering that it's only wired for GE appliances? There must be interface standards. This will help the utility of EMR."

O'Quinn insists that pouring more money into machines can be likened to slapping a band-aid on an open wound that begs for stitches instead.

> There is a big push by the [U.S.] administration to have healthcare organizations move to an electronic medical record (EMR). An EMR certainly has value, but if the overall goal is cost reduction, its implementation should be coordinated with the organization's work flow and financial development. For example, if an organization does not address its work flow issues prior to EMR implementation, it will simply automate inefficiency.
>
> When I worked in manufacturing we used to say, "If you automate a bad process, you will produce bad product very efficiently." An organization also needs to be financially ready for an EMR. For a multihospital system, an EMR costs tens of millions. Implementing one too soon is like investing a large sum of money in a ladder to reach fruit at the top of a tree when low-hanging fruit could have been picked for a fraction of the cost.

O'Quinn makes an interesting point that we should consider. Automating a deficient process is certainly deficient in itself. Thus, what actions could you take to minimize the risk associated with automating poor processes? Just as companies are dying to throw dollars at complex big data healthcare solutions—many without even knowing if they're really ready or not—they simply love automation. The perception exists—automation can make life easier, save the organization substantial costs, and improve the overall quality of healthcare through availability and accuracy.

Before procuring such a solution, clearly defining the end state for performance is vital to implementing a solution effectively and efficiently. First, align the desired end state to the organization's mission and objectives, followed by a thorough analysis of potential options, on both the system/ process requirements (via metrics tied to performance, cost, schedule, and risk) and the capabilities offered by industry for acquisition. Knowing what the system/process *should* look like will subsequently allow you to identify potential solutions that most adequately and appropriately fulfill those specific requirements. Simply, do your analysis before you jump.

Critical Q&A

What is the one process improvement that healthcare in the United States can no longer afford not to make?

Many of the key issues expressed by clinicians and patients involve patient access to care, patient throughput, delays in moving out of ERs, and so forth, and can often be traced to the bed management process. This process involves a number of interdependent, but often uncoordinated, activities involving staff from across the facility, including nurses, admissions and registration, housekeeping, and transportation.

The solutions generally involve enhanced communication and tracking systems and a focus on patient flow. Unfortunately, no one department or leader generally has visibility of the many moving parts. As demand for care continues to increase, and when the unmet pent-up demand for care from the uninsured or underinsured is accommodated through proposed changes in insurance coverage, this one process could be further strained when that demand hits the healthcare delivery system.

—Junell Scheeres

In light of the news about the partnership between Orange in France and Sorin Group in Italy to enable remote cardiac monitoring as an example of telemedicine, will we see this type of care more in the next few years?

There are companies in the U.S. today that have been doing it for five to seven years. One of them is around research that was done by Leapfrog Group, a consortium of the largest purchasers of healthcare in the United States. Companies like FedEx, GM, and Ford got together because they were concerned about what they were spending on healthcare. They found that if you spend a dollar on a banana in Atlanta, you got one thing, and then a dollar somewhere else, you got a rotten banana. They found wide variations in their research. Out of that came six or seven things that were characteristic in the best financial clinical outcomes: use of computerized order entry system, patients' care being directed by intensive care medicine ("intensivists") as opposed to just a doctor or primary care doctor who admitted you, presence of the intensivist around the clock, and then the volume of procedures that the hospital did.

Let's say coronary bypass; the ones that did them the most were the best at that procedure. So the companies went to the organizations like Piedmont Hospital with these top outcomes and demanded that they do these things. One of their paradoxes was that if every hospital decided they would have an intensivist around the clock, it would not be affordable. Let's say the government provided money for it, but the other problem is that our medical schools aren't graduating enough to staff these needs.

I'd like to offer two innovative examples:

1. Philips VISICU, which harnesses telemedicine to drive costs out and improve clinical outcomes through using a proactive care model that provides a solution to physician and nurse shortages while dramatically improving quality of care.
2. Georgia Tech and Emory's project in which they renovated a house on campus with technology that enables and facilitates better interaction with health providers from home; one thing is a pill dispenser tied to a database in the doctor's office. It knows when you took the pill and logs the time.

With these two programs, quantifiable outcomes then became a platform for a lot of disease (like diabetes/glucose meter) management tools.

—Dean Athanassiades

Chapter 5

Trading Hotel Rooms for Sick Beds

Travel overseas is no longer about the exotic reptile voyages or learning about the thousands of plant species interconnected in the rain forest. Add in a liver transplant or a nose job and you have a multitiered vacation that saves time, money, and resources.

Jordan claims the Dead Sea for special sunrays that replenish skin cells and build your immune system. India touts special hip replacement and heart procedures that cost 20 times less than those in the United States. Cuba claims special treatment for night blindness and skin diseases. And Thailand has long been known for gender reassignment.

The book *Medical Tourism in Developing Countries*, by Milica and Karla Bookman, explains:

> While the tourist industry in many developing countries may indeed foster dependency relationships, medical tourism is an exception. It does not raise the dependency concerns that dependency theory so clearly delineates…. Medical tourism in the countries under study tends to be high tech and state of

the art; the facilities are sophisticated and clean; the service is impeccable. Medical tourism is not sold to cruise passengers on a land package, like handicrafts at a port stall. It is not sold on the world markets through large Western multinationals that control the entire vertical production process. It is not cash crop extracted from the land.

As the Bookmans' book also points out, the evidence of foreign investment and international partnerships is overwhelming: In India, foreign capital has gone to new specialty corporate hospitals and state-of-the-art equipment by multinationals. A $40 million cardiac center at Faribadad, the Sir Edward Dunlop Hospital, was established by a consortium of companies from Australia, Canada, and India. Also, a German company has been allowed 90 percent equity ownership for setting up a 200-bed facility in New Delhi. In Mumbai, GMBH of Germany has been given permission for setting up an orthopedic clinic with full ownership. In Jordan, 11 private hospitals have sprung up as a result of these investments. Thailand and Cuba are also origin countries benefiting from the partnerships.

The Bookmans write:

> Yes, it is somewhat glamorized, and often the data for U.S. outbound medical travel is overstated. We believe medical tourism increasingly offers choice to patients seeking 1) lower cost procedures than can be found in their home country (e.g. U.S., where some 80 million un- and under-insured healthcare consumers have been priced out of the healthcare market); 2) higher quality care than can be found in their own country; 3) shorter waiting periods for care (e.g. UK, Canada, Scandinavia, France); 4) to obtain elective surgeries not offered in their own country.

Left Out by Mainstream Media?

During the past decade, health news coverage in the United States has focused primarily on policy, the debate on health reform, specific diseases such as cancer and diabetes, and public health issues such as food contamination and product recalls. The subject of medical tourism has been sparingly covered by larger news organizations with global resources such as CNN International and the *New York Times.*

There is a magazine devoted to the industry not fittingly titled *Medical Tourism Magazine,* which was established in 2007 to advocate a "global healthcare world," and the editors do not apologize for its self-serving articles and advertisements.

Highly specialized research has been published in niche publications such as *Medical News Today,* but you have to look for it. Professor Richard Smith of the London School of Hygiene and Tropical Medicine has been responsible for a lot of the provocative research on cross-border supply of health services, consumption of services abroad, foreign direct investment, and the movement of health professionals.

For instance, according to Smith and colleagues, private patients seeking health services is becoming big business, as noted in hard figures: Thailand is the leading exporter, at over 1 million patients per year and revenues of $615 million, but India is predicted to have revenues of $2.2 billion, Singapore $1.6 billion, and Malaysia $590 million by 2012. It's evident that demand for services abroad is driven by domestic nonavailability, often in specialized treatment areas, which Gez Agolli reiterates. Additionally, low labor costs combined with highly trained medical professionals who were educated in the United States and the UK give these countries a huge cost advantage.

Smith said, "The main constraint on trade is the scarcity of insurance portability. Many national insurance schemes restrict patients seeking foreign service providers when that service is available domestically. In the European Union, for example, although there is portability across member countries for emergency care, elective care needs previous approval from domestic health authorities."

Migration of nurses, doctors, and medical technology innovators to other countries appears to be at the heart of medical tourism becoming a viable option for many Americans in particular. Consider Smith's summary of what he has deemed the "main pathway for health-services trade": Approximately 30 percent of UK doctors are of foreign origin, with India, Ireland, Pakistan, South Africa, and Egypt providing the majority of these. In the United States, Canada, and Australia, about 20 percent of doctors are foreign (many of whom are from the UK).

A result of this cross-border career relocation is that poorer countries have lost doctors, leading to a disproportionate effect on the national stock of skills in those nations. For nurses, low- and middle-income countries provide the majority of foreign nurses working in the UK—in 2002, around half of the 25,602 work permits issued to foreign workers for nursing were to nurses from the Philippines or India.

Just like workers in any other profession, job satisfaction, pay, and career opportunities are among the reasons healthcare workers wish to migrate. Smith notes, "However, the effect of migration on human capital stocks (so-called brain drain) is a cause of concern. The ultimate destination of workers to rich countries, and often the private sector within these countries, has knock-on effects down the chain to public sectors within wealthy nations, private and public sectors in low-income countries, and ultimately the rural areas within poorer countries."

Opposing Views

Zarr opposes the buzz around medical tourism. "We should not be talking about medical tourism in this country. I cannot fundamentally understand why anyone would want to go so far away from home for an important medical procedure. We have the resources here. There are post-operative issues— mainly psychological. The lure of robotics in cardiac procedures will only go so far. You will want to be home resting in your own bed, I guarantee it! If you're only going for cost, there's a simple way to deal with cost. Expand Medicare. Little by little, everyone will be covered."

Gez Agolli didn't wait for any miracle American resources to appear and zap his patients' cancer cells away. He needed treatments that involved innovative strategies that safely attacked the cancerous cells without damaging good cells. Germany and Mexico, rather than the most popular countries for foreign medical services, came to mind.

Agolli explains, "The German and Mexican clinics utilized hyperthermia (heating the body in a controlled setting 105 up to 108 degrees, and then injecting low-dose chemo into the tumor). Ozone therapy intravenously and IPT, lower insulin levels to starve cancer cells, and then inject glucose with the low-dosage chemo as a chaser were also implemented. This procedure eradicates cancer cells (apoptosis) without damaging the good cells. The patients received hope and had the will to fight their disease."

Josef Woodman, author of the book *Patients Beyond Borders,* has heard hundreds of similar stories by physicians like Agolli. As president of Healthy Travel Media, Woodman has toured medical facilities in 22 countries, researching contemporary medical tourism. His comprehensive guide to destination-specific medical treatment is considered to be the most trusted information on healthcare abroad, and has expanded into eight country-specific editions.

Having visited more than 140 medical facilities for the first edition of his book, Woodman is in the position to answer a pressing question that serves as a starting point for the case of medical tourism and its implications: *Should physicians that are educated here in the States stay or contribute elsewhere?*

"That's a matter of personal choice," said Woodman, once a clinical oncologist specializing in prostate cancer. "I know dozens of physicians and healthcare administrators who have elected to serve in other countries for a variety of reasons (e.g., disenfranchised with U.S. healthcare system, philanthropic, et al.). How will this migration or stay affect improvements under the current U.S. administration and beyond? Hard to say. On the one hand, it's a "brain drain" and competitive. On the other, shared research, data, benchmarks, et al., help to raise the bar on healthcare worldwide, which eventually works to the good of all (much in the way the introduction of reliable, improved Japanese automobiles 30 years ago forced the U.S. auto industry out of a model of planned obsolescence)."

Region Snapshot: Cuba

The development of the health sector is noted as a complement to the tourist industry in Cuba. Its marine environment with crystal-clear water and a moderate climate has been pegged as the ultimate advantage in recovery time from any ailment. Cuba combines recreation with cures to improve the quality of life, offering such treatments as thalassotherapy, which consists of combining wind, water, and climate and hydrotherapeutic factors while staying by the sea to recover and improve your health.

Sea baths have been proven as highly beneficial for patients recovering from several diseases and traumas, and the tourist industry has wasted no time in shuffling out brochures promoting places such as San Diego de los Banos, where water is diuretic and rapidly absorbed and eliminated by the human body. The region's resorts tout acupuncture, specialized mud baths, and apitherapy, which uses bee products in medicinal healing.

Perhaps a step beyond what San Diego de los Banos offers, Elguea, located in central Villa Clara province, is famous for its mineral-rich water. A 1,300-square-meter thermal center has three swimming pools of medicinal water, a sauna, a gymnasium, individual baths, a beauty parlor, massage rooms, and doctor's offices.

Catering to its general population, Cuba has a broad medical infrastructure consisting of international clinics, drugstores, optician's shops, and various specialized institutions. More than 280 hospitals, 400 polyclinics, or day clinics, 116 dental clinics, and 1,500 medical establishments make up a broad network to meet the complex needs in the field of human health.

From a systems-oriented perspective, medical tourism offers choice, cost reduction, and innovation. Its promises may seem foreign for those who haven't been put in the predicament to seriously consider traveling thousands of miles away for a procedure. However, from the position of Agolli and others who wouldn't hesitate to send their patients on a plane for treatment, the quest to solve a medical problem and heal their patient outweighs fear of the unknown. Even dating back over a decade, medical tourism is certainly not new to insurers offering plans that promote this lower-cost approach. Whether you look at this as a great alternative to effective healthcare, it's nonetheless an option. But, one that should make healthcare organizations interested and motivated in finding ways for reducing cost to the patient, while providing the best care possible.

Critical Q&A

> If everyone knew that a $200,000 heart procedure in the United States costs $10,000 in India, what would be the reasons for not seeking the treatment there?
>
> Personal xenophobia and professional protectionism. Many patients just can't see themselves traveling

to a strange country and culture for care, and thus
no amount of savings is sufficient incentive. Often
a patient interested in medical travel will be talked
out of it by a family member or his or her physician/
specialists. Also, liability, quality assurance, and con-
tinuity of care can be huge obstacles (perceived and
actual) to crossing borders for care.

Slowly, the infrastructure is being built that will
address each of these concerns, but for now, the
onus is on the patient to take the time and effort to
become informed. That's often too large a burden for
the average U.S. healthcare consumer. Medical travel
is still much more common outside the U.S., e.g., in
the European Union and Asia, where cross-border
healthcare travel is commonplace.

—Josef Woodman

Should physicians that are educated here in the States stay
or contribute elsewhere? How will this migration or stay
affect improvements under the Obama administration?

We currently license thousands of foreign-trained
medical graduates in this country because there are
not enough training sites or medical school seats to
produce the physicians, particularly primary care
physicians, we need to care for our population.
Regardless of who stays where, there is no sign that
anything the current administration has proposed
has a chance of improving healthcare.

The administration has passed a law that changes
the way that healthcare is paid for, and some of the
aspects of that law have merit. I am not aware of
anything in the law that really impacts how care
will be delivered. The cost to primary care physicians to deliver care to Medicaid patients exceeds

what Medicaid pays for that care. Adding millions of people to the Medicaid rosters without fundamentally changing how physicians are paid for their services is not likely to actually provide healthcare for anyone.

—Donald Campbell, MD

Chapter 6

Insured or Imagined?

Laurence J. Kotlikoff is one of the nation's leading experts on fiscal policy, national saving, and personal finance. He also has a lot to say about financial problems related to the U.S. health system, often dissecting the guts of the insurance business.

Kotlikoff begins his book *The Healthcare Fix*, which outlines the approach of universal insurance for all Americans, with: "The status quo, we're conditioned to believe, is the safe bet, the conservative option, the riskless alternative. But when the status quo involves driving off a cliff, maintaining course is the risky, radical, indeed suicidal choice. The United States is now engaged in precisely this behavior: perpetuating a suicidal status quo. Its policies, primarily those connected with Medicare, Medicaid, and the rest of the healthcare system, are driving the country to fiscal, financial, and economic ruin. The only question is when the crash will occur and who will be in the passenger seats."

Does the insurance business hold this much responsibility in our country's economy? Are the companies to blame for escalating costs? Can they practice tighter administrative control and limit demands placed on employers? Should there be many different plan options and competing companies or one blanket system from which all citizens can receive some form of health insurance?

There is simply not enough bandwidth to answer all the questions that need to be addressed on the industry that health insurance is. However, we must get to the stage in which common ground is shared among all people within the cycle of care and recognize what favorable roles insurance does and can play in a future state of healthcare.

The insurance business is a confusing, chaotic picture for so many of us, though it's such an essential component of our state of health. Not understanding its intricacies and common language is extremely dangerous for each of us. People are inflamed when experiencing spiked rates or getting their COBRA subsidy cut, but did they truly understand what they were paying for before?

Scheeres offered, "The ongoing challenge in the insurance system is the debate between proactive healthcare management and reactive healthcare interventions. The current insurance system rewards and reimburses care for services."

Along the lines of this conjecture, Scheeres insisted that in order to reduce costs, one of three things has to happen:

- Less demand for services. (The White House estimates demand for services provided by the Patient Protection and Affordable Care Act of 2010 will increase coverage by an estimated 32 million lives by 2019.)
- Reduce cost per case, which may be possible with improved adherence to clinical best practices and support of evidence-based medicine and coverage of screening and early detection.
- Change the need for services, which would most likely result from changes in lifestyle and rewards/incentives based on positive lifestyle choices. The insurance system would need to be restructured to support and reward proactive health management.

"Part of the justification for offsetting the costs of the Patient Protection and Affordable Care Act of 2010 is the expectation that Medicare and Medicaid costs associated with fraud and abuse will be reduced," said Scheeres.

> According to the Healthcare Financial Management Association, "the costing and pricing competencies of healthcare organizations is increasingly coming to the forefront as providers move toward clinical process reengineering and as payment systems evolve." Pay-for-performance based on clinical outcomes and episode-based reimbursements driven by changes in the payment systems will put greater emphasis on the cost and quality implications of process improvement activities.
>
> Industrial engineers leading process reengineering efforts will need to be able to ensure only legitimate cases are submitted to insurance companies for reimbursement and help organizations put into place the ways and means to detect potential fraud. They will also need to help teams demonstrate return on investment anticipated and achieved by process improvement projects.

Doctors like Agolli are not convinced that the sweeping changes Scheeres and others say are possible will infiltrate insurance companies as long as they are in business strictly for financial gain. He said:

> They are removed from the emotional side of providing healthcare. It is strictly business! My experience has been that we need insurance for catastrophic events. An accident in which hospitalization is required can bankrupt a family. Therefore, it is imperative to protect yourself and your family. This is where insurance is extremely valuable.

However, when treating chronic disorders, insurance companies will only pay for allopathic treatments and medications. They have not embraced the wellness-and-prevention concept.

In fairness to insurance companies, why should they? Most customers are not loyal and will change insurance carriers every two years. Why should an insurance company invest in your prevention when you will leave them in two years? The bottom line is that the entire medical system is set up for failure. We have been conditioned to believe that someone else should pay for our healthcare. Healthcare is not a right (except for accidents or urgent care). Healthcare should be viewed as a personal responsibility to take care of one's own temple and honor it.

One of the most motivated groups of professionals to carry its voice throughout the healthcare debate has been the Physicians for a National Health Program (PNHP). With a membership of more than 17,000 physicians who support a single-payer national health insurance program, the organization has shared compelling state-by-state data on the uninsured since 2005.

The centerpiece of talking points in various interviews and discussions, here are a few of the findings that PNHP released during 2009 on the uninsured:

■ In Massachusetts, where an individual mandate health reform law was passed in 2006, at least 352,000 people, or 5.5 percent of the population, remained uninsured in 2008. That number was actually higher than the number of uninsured in 2007, before strict enforcement of the individual and employer mandates went into effect.

Dr. Steffie Woolhandler, professor of medicine at Harvard Medical School and cofounder of PNHP clarified, "Today's numbers show that plans that require people to

buy private insurance don't work. Obama's plan to replicate Massachusetts' reform nationally risks failure on a
massive scale."

■ Woolhandler said job losses in the recession, and the
corresponding loss of health coverage, are inadequately
reflected in the new data. An estimated 2.6 million people
lost their jobs in 2008, most of them toward the end of
the year.
■ Census officials cited a drop of 1.1 million in the number
of persons who were covered by employer-based insurance, continuing an eight-year trend. Whereas 64 percent
of Americans had employer-based coverage in 1999, only
58.5 percent had such coverage in 2008.
■ McCanne noted that the Census Bureau was once again
silent on the pervasive problem of underinsurance.
People are usually defined as underinsured if they spend
10 percent or more of their income (or 5 percent if they
are low-income) on out-of-pocket medical expenses in the
course of a year.
  "Not having health insurance, or having poor quality
insurance that doesn't protect you from financial hard-
ship in the face of medical need, is a source of mounting
stress, anguish, and poor medical outcomes for people
across our country," McCanne said.

He also noted that a recent study showed 62 percent of
personal bankruptcies in the United States are now linked to
medical bills or illness. It almost seems that getting a patient
to health to then be faced with bankruptcy and a new—
potentially more dangerous—lifestyle certainly does not help
prevention and wellness, or the cost of care to drop.

"Doctors are very frustrated with billing and going through
hoops for basic things," added Zarr. "Doctors fill out so much
paperwork for insurance companies and deal with a dozen
different ones. To get approval for an MRI for a child that

has a suspected brain tumor is senseless. Even with Medicaid years ago, the intention was good—case management—but we came to see the negative side. Most doctors don't want their services to be free, but there is a tax system that can work to bring access to everyone. Then you pay a decent wage to physicians for their services and do not make the reimbursement process complicated, like it is today. It has forced some doctors to take cash only."

Medicaid and Medicare

In these days of confusing one over the other or questioning how long one or both will even be sustainable for years to come, note the fundamental difference between Medicaid and Medicare. Medicaid is a federally funded program that provides healthcare for low-income individuals and families. The program was set up by the federal government, but is administered on a state-by-state basis. Everyone over the age of 65 may qualify for Medicaid, but other groups of people may too, including pregnant women, children under the age of 18, and people with certain types of disabilities. However, to qualify, your income must also be below a certain limit, as defined on a state-by-state basis.

Medicare is also a federal program, but is specifically for people 65 and over who are no longer working. Medicare is an entitlement program: the only criteria for entry are that you be over the age of 65 and have paid employment or self-employment taxes while working. Medicare provides insurance that covers inpatient and outpatient hospital visits, doctor's visits, and some preventative services (Medicare Parts A and B). In addition, Medicare Part D provides prescription drug coverage. There is also a privately administered type of Medicare known as Part C (or Medicare Advantage). Medicare Advantage usually provides more personalized or extensive health coverage.

According to *USA Today*, one in six Americans is now taking advantage of government antipoverty programs, including more than 50 million on Medicaid. As for Medicare, the number of users are only a few thousand less.

Without a doubt, the combined pair is fraught with issues that could be eased with process improvement. A system that many millions of people share could never be flawless, but the reason that several of our nation's presidents have been fixated on making them better is the toll that inefficiencies have taken on taxpayers, doctors, and recipients—billions of dollars annually in price gouges on pharmaceuticals and medical supplies and equipment. In this maze, there is the patient.

With the help of Scheeres, who has built her career on developing custom solutions to guide executives and teams in achieving breakthrough results and validated outcomes, let's follow a fictitious patient (but one that's representative of the actual population we're referring to) through a few scenarios related to insurance coverage:

> Uninsured Patient needs a medical device.
> Several factors influence where Patient may receive medical care. The primary factor involved in receiving in-patient care is the medical necessity of the admission based on the physician's description of need. This is a requirement regardless of insurance coverage. Even when medical necessity is confirmed, one of the first activities for the admission office is to notify and obtain "authorization" from Patient's insurance company.
>
> In this case, Patient requires a life-saving procedure and does not have insurance, so the admission office will consider placement options based on the facility's mission and status. In for-profit settings, Patient will be stabilized and may be transferred for treatment to a not-for-profit or public health facility for as long as the medical necessity warrants.

Where appropriate, the facility's admission office may be able to work with Patient and her family regarding their financial obligation and to help them set up a payment plan based on their ability to pay.

Personal circumstances may qualify Patient for medical reimbursement programs such as Medicare, Medicaid, or Charity Care. Many not-for-profit and faith-based healthcare facilities have charitable foundations to help meet this need. Not-for-profit hospitals receive tax advantages and other incentives when they care for a disproportionate share of under- or uninsured patients and charity care write-offs.

Physician costs and settlement are between Patient and her provider, and are not generally included in the in-patient costs. In recent years, healthcare facilities have begun employing their own physicians to help manage the in-patient stay, including focused attention on medical documentation and length-of-stay issues that contribute to the hospital's revenue cycle and financial viability.

Uninsured Patient requires a hospital stay and further treatment.

Once Patient's admission is made by a physician, case managers in the healthcare facility monitor evidence of medical necessity throughout her hospital stay based on provider notes and advancement along Patient's care plan. Part of monitoring this plan is an assessment of Patient's ability to manage further care in the in-patient or out-patient setting. The clinical team provides ongoing assessments, and decisions are made each day whether to continue her admission.

Each case has an expected length of stay based on planned/completed medical activities. Patient's progress is tracked against this expectation and adjustments are made based on mitigating circumstances, usually supported by additional medical documentation of need. The care provided is translated into financial reimbursement based on the payment system codes used by the Centers for Medicare and Medicaid Services' (CMS) and the discharge diagnosis of Patient's clinical condition.

The diagnosis related group (DRG) code reported by the physician and supported by documentation in the medical record will be used to request reimbursement from the payer (private and government). Disparity between procedures performed or length of stay and the discharge diagnosis can result in reimbursement gaps and potentially denial of claims.

In October of 2013, CMS will change from its twenty-seven-year-old ICD-9 system (with 13,000 diagnosis codes and 3,000 procedure codes) to the new ICD-10 pay-for-performance system with over 60,000 diagnosis codes and 72,000 procedure codes. This increased specificity will require a more precise level of documentation and data mining to understand which services and procedures impact clinical outcomes as well as reimbursement.

> *Patient had some insurance, but it*
> *ran out during her hospital stay.*

In order for Patient to remain in the hospital, a valid physician order must exist. Stays beyond the anticipated length of stay associated with the medical condition must be validated on a case-by-case basis and are followed closely by the clinical and administrative staff. If no medical necessity is warranted, Patient will be discharged. In for-profit facilities, when medical necessity exists, but insurance coverage lapses,

Patient may be transferred to a public or non-profit setting, where care or payment arrangements will be made with Patient and her family if she has one.

How Engineers Can Help Patients

For situations like the three described above, industrial engineers have helped healthcare facilities examine their admission, authorization, documentation, and case management processes to support financial reimbursement of care.

Changes to access to care due to the Patient Protection and Affordable Care Act of 2010 will likely generate an even greater need to confirm coverage and work out information transfer relationships with third-party payers. Not to mention the requirement for substantial improvements, training, and communication during this period.

Process improvement consultants—whether internal or external to the organization—should begin to help healthcare organizations anticipate changes in demand and associated processes needed to confirm coverage.

Additionally, engineers can partner with the health information services and clinical informatics departments to facilitate this transition. Consider methods such as those mentioned earlier on IT systems/processes. These engineers can help guide a detailed examination of documentation behaviors of care providers as well as streamline and optimize current medical reporting and financial transaction processes. They can also ensure transactions successfully transition between medical records and financial information systems.

Steve Bent, a legal expert in the Life Sciences Division at Foley Law, explains that the federal government sets pricing standards for drugs and devices, but companies are trying to get those prices changed, knowing the reimbursement system will rapidly change with new laws.

"The Medicare-Medicaid system covers 20 percent of certain areas of the cost," said Bent. "My generation is getting old enough that they are using the system. How this is handled is a big issue in the future. We choose to use the reimbursement system as price control. People are urging more aggressive use of this system. In Europe and Canada, the system is less expensive including the devices—whether that will happen here is unlikely, but this is part of healthcare reform for medical imaging, for example. We will have a standard for why and how medical imaging is used because it is an expensive part of the process, and that is a direct control on how medical care is administered."

Bent also acknowledged the other standards that will be put forth—what doctors can and can't do regarding technology. Pharma has been highly regulated, but the medical device manufacturers have had an easier time, and those days may be over. The medical device sector will be held much the same way under scrutiny. Heightened regulatory burden will take many different forms.

How are process improvement gurus, including the insurance industry, in their pleas to overhaul the nation's healthcare system? Considering its size and complexities, how does its intricacies relate to the power of tools like Six Sigma? How are they addressing this "regulatory burden" that Bent speaks of?

Scheeres referenced a report published by Moody's Investors Service in May 2010. "Transforming Not-for-Profit Healthcare in the Era of Reform" indeed suggested that healthcare systems will need to invest in information technology to help them reduce costs and improve quality. One of the areas where industrial engineers are working with insurance companies, both public and private, is claims processing. That's a big start, given the expectation that claims management will lead to reductions in fraud and abuse and the upcoming demand for services is likely to create a surge in claims.

Scheeres added, "Experts agree that healthcare organizations can expect greater transparency of information as well as changes in reimbursement based on clinical outcomes and charges associated with the delivery of care. Industrial engineers can support this need by facilitating projects that result in compliance to best clinical practices and evidence-based medicine. They can also lead information system implementation and integration projects as electronic medical records and other supporting information systems are put into practice."

Here, other experts weigh in with their definitions and prescriptions for what health insurance should be.

The Expert Is In

"In the interest of pharmaceutical and insurance companies, use legislation to force transparency and remove barriers to competition," O'Quinn suggested. "The perception seems to be that these industries make an exorbitant profit. Perhaps that is true. One thing is for certain, little Johnny is not going to sell his lemonade for less than $10 a glass until little Judy starts selling her lemonade for 50¢ a glass. Let's make sure little Johnny has not imposed some artificial barriers for the competition."

It's true—prices generally do not go down without cause or reason. Who would think that healthcare costs are even negotiable—that I, as an insurance provider, actually negotiate, successfully, mind you, the cost of a small paper pill cup or some procedure. The fact that this can be done and costs, justified or not, somewhere in the system allow patients to realize substantial costs passed by someone in the supply chain. It's clearly a concern, and one in dire need of improvement. As an improvement "guru," I was taught to never pass unnecessary costs on to the consumer. Why should healthcare be any different?

In her book *Who Killed Healthcare?* Herzlinger sets up five precise goals of consumer-driven care:

- Consumer-driven insurers will design consumer-friendly insurance policies that give you the benefits, coverage, and doctors you want at a price you are willing to pay.
- Consumer-friendly hospitals will take part in integrated teams that give you everything you need for your disease or disability.
- Consumer-driven employers will direct their HR staff to give you back the part of your salary that they used to buy your health insurance, and then they will help you choose from the many new varieties of policies that become available.
- The U.S. Congress will pass laws that enable you to buy your health insurance with tax-free income, help to create information about the quality and prices of medical care providers, and transfer money to the poor so they can shop for health insurance like all other Americans.
- Academics will research how to make this consumer-driven market work better, just like the Nobel Prize-winning economists who help to uncover inefficiencies in the financial markets and devise ways to correct them.

"The solution for our healthcare system is complex," said Agolli.

However, I believe that through strong leadership, positive change can occur. From my perspective, we need to create a consumer-driven healthcare system by training all doctors on prevention, wellness, nutrition, diet, stress reduction, exercise, herbal medicine, homeopathy, Chinese medicine, auyervadic, naturopathy, osteopathy, and chiropratic. Use medications only when necessary to treat acute infections, trauma, and certain chronic disorders only when wellness and nutrition has been used as first line of defense.

This change will involve abolishing the insurance industry, changing the role of the FDA (instead of just evaluating research of drug companies). All new medications will be researched by an independent scientific team that work for a government agency. Therefore, only medications that are scientific based that do no harm will be approved. There will be no financial incentive for the drugs to be pushed through.

Hospital care should be socialized and funded by our government but managed by an independent MSO (manage service organization). The funds will be procured through a series of excise taxes on tobacco, alcohol, junk foods. We can raise the funds painlessly through innovative programs. No reason to increase personal income. Doctor visits, treatments and diagnostics should be paid for through private healthcare savings, private insurance, or self-pay. The government should have programs to match funds depending on income level. Therefore, no one is left behind and we will teach our citizens regardless of race, class or education level that their health is their responsibility. I will guarantee that we will have a better outcome costing less in the long run.

Finally, Scheeres, who earned a PhD in healthcare administration, said, "I think the only way the private sector healthcare industry in general will significantly change is when consumers (of all income levels) are able to personally select their physicians and healthcare delivery facilities. As long as that choice is still controlled predominantly by the insurance providers, the industry will continue to be divided in its loyalties and reliant on those who pay the bills (the government, private and publicly funded insurers) for their compliance with healthcare delivery expectations.

> The acceleration of government-driven healthcare will lead to a rise in boutique medicine creating a significant difference between the healthcare delivery experienced by the "haves" and the "have-nots." The healthcare delivery system providing services for the "haves" will be able to attract the best talent, the leading technology, and the premium facilities. These systems will differentiate the patient experience as well as the desired outcomes.

Critical Q&A

Can you describe your experience with insurance companies as a whole in relationship to the patient care you facilitate?

> As a whole, I do not feel that insurance companies stand in the way of providing adequate healthcare to their insured. As a matter of fact, a few, like Anthem, try to provide medical management services to attempt to improve outcomes for cancer patients or others with complicated illnesses.

> **—James Rickert**

Is the Obama administration moving in the right direction to improve healthcare?

> No, and not because the effort isn't sincere, but mostly because the vision hasn't been clearly articulated. Before $1 of taxpayer money is drawn off in a new direction, I think it is imperative for the

government leaders to present a clear and specific view of the future state healthcare system to include the relationship between private, for-profit, not-for-profit, and government care and the interactions across the system, between resources providing care, the systems delivering care, and the entities funding care.

—Junell Scheeres

Chapter 7

The Classroom: Where Medicine Begins

In earlier times, many careers in medicine began in an anatomy laboratory filled with fresh corpses from the nearby morgue. Their studies of saving lives ironically started with being surrounded by the dead, a grisly departure from ordinary life. Some of them had obtained a bachelor's degree in a completely different field: music, political science, English. Then miraculously, the need to serve medicine entered the picture. Anatomy, physiology, and biochemistry replaced everything they were taught in liberal arts.

Acceptance into medical school is big business. It's also the dinner conversation among families for many years to come when a member makes the fateful announcement.

Some of the graduates will go on to become surgeons—perfectionists whose operations are pure examples of clarity and absence of wasted motion. Every move with their hands holding instruments is deliberate. Every soft-spoken instruction the next calculated step to completing a successful procedure. They know that anatomy is the science of the body's structure and the relation of its parts; physiology is the science that looks at the functions of the living organism and its parts.

You cannot make achievements in the surgical theater without practicing both simultaneously.

Medical schools are frequently left out of the language of healthcare. If the medical mindsets and skills are fostered behind these doors, it's a mystery why.

Zarr offered, "In college, students have lofty goals of helping others, but the reality is they have accrued a debt for education for $200,000 to $500,000. They realize that the quickest way to get out of that debt is to be a specialist. People are trying to do what's best for the health of the country, but circumstances weigh against them. Students who go into primary care should be relieved of debt. This is one solution to the health system problem. Education is mainly taught by specialists. It's exciting to see the latest technology, but learning to care for a diabetic is also exciting, and this needs to be encouraged. Medical education debt is a real issue."

Campbell also emphasized the debt issue in his thoughts on the state of medical education and if equity in care is a learned priority in the classroom.

> There is nothing I am aware of in medical training today that is addressing racial and income disparities. We still produce physicians who prefer to practice in communities where they will be paid for their services. We will not see a change in this pattern, in my view, until we do something about the cost of medical education.... Given the option to earn over $250,000 a year as a specialist in an urban setting or $125,000 in a rural area doing primary care, I can't see any change in who practices where in the near term.

New Faces of Medical Education

Interestingly, there are significant partnerships between U.S.-based universities and professional organizations in other parts of the world that exist to address challenges with the state of public health globally. Some of them are focusing on innovation in medical school curricula, medical technology, mental health, and the cost of education. Unfortunately, the kernels of information and outstanding projects that they're working on just aren't well publicized.

Stephen Simpson is the director of life sciences at Science Foundation Ireland, a foundation of scientific excellence in Ireland that was formed eight years ago when the government decided that the country needed a boost in communications and technology in life sciences.

Simpson is among hundreds of program directors that attends the Bio International Convention annually. The convention is an exclusive forum that features thought leaders in biotechnology, politicians, and innovators on the cutting edge of pharmaceuticals, medical equipment, and yes, medical education. Past speakers include President George W. Bush, President Bill Clinton, Michael J. Fox, Sir Elton John, Her Majesty Queen Noor of Jordan, and General Colin Powell, among many others. As a result, security is high and interviews with press are sparse.

For the purpose of this book, Simpson talked about a few of the projects that Science Foundation Ireland and the United States are involved in.

> We have the U.S.–Ireland program that involves the north of Ireland, the Republic of Ireland and the United States in which we have identified specific disease areas like cystic fibrosis and diabetes to explore. The research undergoes peer review, and once that passes peer review, the three countries' funding moves it forward. We would like to have an extension of international partnerships to link a researcher in Ireland. We would fund the research, but we would have short-term fellowships in which Irish researchers go to the lab and vice versa.

We also have a program that allows any researcher from any part of the planet to come over to Ireland for the maximum of 12 months and work for a profit. A student from Georgia Tech or the University of Arizona would come and spend 6 to 12 months in an Irish lab. University of Dublin, Trinity would host that person, so there are all sorts of programs that we are designed to support globally. There are strategically important disease areas we're focused on.

Bench-to-Bedside Approach

According to Simpson, specific programs are emphasizing the practice of *translational research*, which brings research together from various types of scientists and shares it with clinicians. The action behind this education is having the right network of clinicians and linking those to the research and the right companies to push it through the translational pipeline in which the population will benefit. The teams can then witness the research coming into the practice.

This concept, or practice for many now, raises the question: How much research really benefits patients? To show its commitment to translational research, the National Institutes of Health launched the Clinical and Translational Science Awards Consortium in 2006. The consortium began with 12 academic health centers located throughout the nation and expanded to 46 within three years. By 2012, NIH said, approximately 60 institutions will be connected to "energize the discipline of clinical and translational science."

As member institutes, they have pledged to forge a uniquely transformative, novel, and integrative academic home for clinical and translational science that has the consolidated resources to: (1) captivate, advance, and nurture a cadre of well-trained multi- and interdisciplinary investigators and research teams; (2) create an incubator for innovative research tools and information technologies; and (3) synergize multidisciplinary and interdisciplinary clinical and translational research and researchers to catalyze the application of new knowledge and techniques to clinical practice at the front lines of patient care.

In a press release issued by NIH on July 14, 2009, highlights on progress for a two-year span were announced on disease areas and conditions including cancer, neurological diseases, diabetes, and obesity.

For an excellent example of a multidisciplinary team, you need only look to the translational research group that NIH has established to bring forth its mission of applying new knowledge and techniques in healthcare: a computer scientist from the National Institute of Alcohol Abuse and Alcoholism, a chief from the National Institute on Deafness and Other Communications Disorders, a pharmacologist in contraceptive and reproductive health, and researchers specializing in aging, stroke, blood diseases, and skin diseases, among others.

NIH issued the following statement, summarizing its stance on translational research:

> Scientists are increasingly aware that this bench-to-bedside approach to translational research is really a two-way street. Basic scientists provide clinicians with new tools for use in patients and for assessment of their impact, and clinical researchers make novel observations about the nature and progression of disease that often stimulate basic investigations. Translational research has proven to be a powerful process that drives the clinical research engine. However, a stronger research infrastructure could strengthen and accelerate this critical part of the clinical research enterprise. The NIH Roadmap attempts to catalyze translational research in various ways.

Simpson also noted that Harvard Catalyst, which brings together the intellectual context, clinical expertise, and technology of Harvard University and its affiliates and partners to "reduce the burden of human illness," is the perfect example of the power behind translational research.

The Catalyst's mission is:

> What is missing is a systematic way for investigators from disparate disciplines and institutions to find each other and form teams, to gain open access to tools and technologies, and to obtain seed funding to embark upon new areas of investigation. This demands a systematic effort to remove the barriers and obstacles to cross-institutional collaboration. A catalyst lowers the barriers to reaction, and thus speeds a reaction that would normally have occurred at a much slower rate. Speeding the reduction of human illness is the only function of the Harvard Catalyst.

The Catalyst's emphasis on benchmarking discovery alone spans the four tiers that its network fosters: basic scientific discovery translated to humans, clinical insights translated to patients, implications for healthcare practice translated to practice, and implications for population health translated to improved global health.

Explained on Pathfinder, a pictorial rich media website linked to Harvard Catalyst that's filled with case studies and sample training techniques from each tier, translational research is depicted as a modern and exciting atlas of healthcare learning and practicum. And "excitement" is exactly what U.S. medical education needs, said Simpson.

Simpson added, "There are lots of young people who would love to do research, and we not do enough to excite them and encourage them. We can do more to promote science itself and the relationship with medicine. It is so important in humanity as well as the socioeconomic vibrancy in any country."

Engineering Medicine

Debusk acknowledges the importance of research that is coupled with an approach in the classroom that emphasizes how healthcare workers can function as a team and work together.

> We need to move healthcare from a craft culture to a system culture, and education could help this process. More emphasis should be on techniques like lean and process improvements, with incentives for hospitals with high quality, low cost, and high patient satisfaction, with less emphasis on specific technologies like EMR.

Because healthcare worldwide depends on more services for less cost, industrial engineers in medical sectors meet unique criteria for doing specific jobs. They've had to learn physiology, chemistry for simulation, and data mining for cost modeling. Once they possess a working knowledge of life science, which Simpson advocates, their skills are applied to six tasks, ranging from reducing costs and standardizing operations to streamlining processes and recommending automation solutions.

Some physicians are not seeing these advanced education practices in the clinical setting. "As much as I would like to say that quality improvement is a part of patient management, physicians are just now becoming able to consider quality improvement by looking at data from patient encounters," insisted Campbell. "There is no track record of quality improvement in the clinical setting. Advances in medicine have been driven solely by research in clinical trials. With data available from EHRs, we may begin to see some real quality improvement in the clinical practice setting. Lean is certainly one of the quality improvement techniques that will be useful."

Agreed. Knowing this, these concepts should be shared at the academic institutional level, and ingrained in healthcare institutions. Improving patient care is not just represented as a new, safer means for removing a particular organ or applying some treatment, but it also extends to patient stays (more time equals more cost to the patient), balancing of staff to promote effectiveness, efficiency, and error reduction, and many other areas. We must move beyond the "way things have always been done" and egos, and realize that better quality lies with improvement.

Exemplary Partnership

An alliance designed to improve the care of approximately 1.2 million veterans began in 2009 between Northeastern University and the New England Veterans Affairs (VA). According to James Benneyan, executive director of the New England Healthcare Engineering Partnership (NEHCEP), concentration areas span access, waits and delays, safety, optimal care, efficiency, equity, and effectiveness. It's no coincidence that these are the same priorities identified by the U.S. Institute of Medicine and the National Academy of Engineering.

Funded by $3.4 million annually in grant and matching funding from the Department of Veteran Affairs, NEHCEP is one of four Veterans Engineering Research Centers. Partners include the Massachusetts Institute of Technology, Worcester Polytechnic Institute, and several VA Centers of Excellence.

"The main objective in the long term is to create capacity within the VA, and that will spill over into the national healthcare system," Benneyan told *Industrial Engineer* magazine upon the announcement of the partnership. He is also a professor of industrial and mechanical engineering at Northeastern. "The VA was chosen very carefully, at least for me to get involved in, because it is the largest healthcare system and one of our best healthcare systems that will play a role in the discussion on whatever happens with national healthcare. The idea is to cross-educate healthcare practitioners and industrial engineers about each other's domain, and that is not going on enough anywhere. There are pockets of this integration, but these pockets need to be much broader and deeper."

Located within the Boston VA Healthcare System, NEHCEP serves the New England network of 8 medical centers and 37 community-based outpatient clinics. In conjunction with full-time leadership positions at the centers, the alliance is also developing innovative interdisciplinary academic programs for engineers and healthcare professionals in order to present solutions that marry their skills and principles. Advanced mathematical and computer modeling methods to analyze, improve, and optimize various types of processes are being used frequently in the programs.

Key to this interdisciplinary partnership is the union of experienced professionals and their valuable resources in the business world with talented students and their professors who have a keen sense of the emerging needs of healthcare today. The team, or various teams (depending on how you define the consortium of universities and organizations), has created a "community of practice," where participation leverages not only a large dose of monetary funding, but collective experience, exploratory and translational research, and developmental capabilities.

Put on Your Scrubs and Learn How to Communicate

Indicating the significance of communications excellence in healthcare settings, note a multipronged collaboration that was put in motion to help 8,000 medical doctors and other healthcare providers improve their interpersonal and communications skills. All initiatives were designed to improve patient outcomes.

Corporate Performance Consultants, Inc., which specializes in organizational performance improvement among healthcare companies, was selected for a groundbreaking project with the American Academy of Physical Medicine and Rehabilitation (AAPM&R), the official medical association committed to advancing the specialty of physical medicine and rehabilitation, and WE MOVE, an ACCME-accredited educational provider specializing in neurology and psychiatry.

According to the group, improvement in communications among doctors, their colleagues, patients, and family members has been demonstrated to increase patient adherence to doctors' recommendations by up to 19 percent.

Using a media-rich interactive model for learning, the program challenged physicians to consider the science of how they communicate, as opposed to just what they communicate, to identify the style of communication they generally employ in patient interactions and to learn to recognize the language cues associated with other communication styles so that they modify their responses to optimize a patient's ability to understand.

David Berube, professor of communications and nanostudies and technology studies at North Carolina State University, has spoken on water applications and nanomedicine as the two areas that healthcare will benefit most from nanotechnology. His specialties are risk communication, public engagement, and media analysis. Berube received a $1.4 million grant from the National Science Foundation to explore the public's understanding of science and technology and devise communication strategies and tactics.

As such, his students are learning a different language in public health that bridges the gap between the research side and how medical technology flows through the type of pipeline that Simpson refers to. Berube insists that the public must be invited to the party in which information about the practices and tools that will affect their lives is being circulated.

"Half of the people in the scientific implications world aren't natural scientists; we are social scientists," said Berube. "We do different types of work. Scientists like us because we use data as well. Someone came up with the word *scientitiate* (I love the word). The concept is about making people science-literate so they can actually engage in meaningful dialogue with people in science and engineering. Unfortunately, this is not happening. The general public has already decided it does not want to do science. People in science/education work from this false assumption: teach people science and they will support science. They believe they can make the public partially literate in science, but that process can be countereffective, counterproductive.

> The public tends to react negatively to risk data because they only have some information and really don't want much more. Some of the data is communicated by PR professionals, which is terrible. They market rather than engage the public. The engagement is incomplete, and there is little positive reinforcement. For most people in the natural sciences, communications are outsourced. The public is completely outside of the process; they have no idea what is happening in processes.

Berube adds that science is expensive, and you need a public that is willing to have its tax dollars allocated toward it. Educating the public is crucial to receiving a supportive infrastructure. Beyond classrooms like Berube's, how does the United States fare in the level of communication needed to endorse healthcare developments like nanotechnology?

Berube responded, "I'm a little impressed with some of the experiments that take place in the European Union, especially Germany and the UK. Italy is picking up too. They are trying different experiments with the public, they're learning more and more about how the public reacts, what stories they want us to tell, what they will react to."

With the mission of overcoming barriers that can keep patients from taking their medications according to instructions or going to the emergency room when they would be better served in primary care, the U.S. Department of Health and Human Services (HHS) devised its own communications course that anyone can complete online—for free. Unified Health Communication: Addressing Health Literacy, Cultural Competency, and Limited English has helped more than 4,000 healthcare professionals and students improve patient-provider communication.

Reiterating the need for literacy that Berube has advocated for in his classrooms and other platforms, HHS states that *health literacy* is defined to the degree to which individuals have the capacity to obtain, process, and understand basic health information needed to make appropriate health decisions and services needed to prevent or treat illness. Ongoing workshops, newsletters, and other external communications supported by the Board on Public Health and Public Health Practice from the Institute of Medicine continue to promote health literacy on dozens of topics, such as HIV/AIDS programs, maternal and child health, rural health, and organ transplantation.

When asked if current coursework is keeping pace with demands placed on physicians by new rules and regulations, Campbell doubts that real synergy between the two worlds is imminent.

> The requirements under the new Affordable Care Act remain so vague that there is no way to structure education that presumes to meet these requirements. Medical schools are now beginning to teach teamwork and communication, which will help physicians to be better caregivers and coaches to their patients. The pace of change in the medical school curriculum

is very slow because medical schools continue to be funded based on the same academic/research paradigm that has been in place for the past several decades. Until that changes, there will be no substantive change in the curriculum.

Stress Nature over Pharma

Agolli, who has built his practice on naturopathic medicine, urges that medical schools must steer away from relationships with pharmaceutical companies and forge cross-cultural partnerships that emphasize holistic health, which focuses on all facets of human functioning (psychological, physical, social, mental).

"All medical schools must train their physicians about wellness, diet, exercise, detoxification, exercise," Agolli explained. "Teach our physicians to be teachers instead of drug pushers. We are a nation of instant gratification, and our doctors feed that problem by prescribing too many medications. We are the only nation besides New Zealand to advertise pharmaceuticals on television. This forces the doctor to prescribe meds that are not needed because the public is brainwashed into believing that need for drugs. Medications should be used to treat acute problems, not chronic conditions. We are taught through the philosophy of Hippocrates to first, do no harm! Prescribing drugs for every condition leads to irreparable damages in many patients' lives. Teaching wellness and prevention with personal responsibility is number 1!"

Finally, how would Simpson rate his own health system in Ireland? Having lived in several different countries, his answer stretches beyond Irish land.

I would say that there is some excellence in terms of expertise and quality of healthcare. But I come from the UK, where it is free, so I think in that area, the UK has the upper hand. In clinical care, with particular diseases, Ireland does well, but in other areas, we have to catch up. Aside from my professional roles, I give a personal perspective. I feel strongly that Ireland must move toward a national health system. It's a complicated system on who gets covered. In the States, I think that there is a two-tiered system. In Ireland, even if you don't have health insurance, you will get taken care of in the same standard with someone who does have health insurance. Money will buy you speed there, but not a different level of quality. I also lived in the U.S. and had the most serious need of healthcare in my life in Boston for an operation, and the experience was exceptional. I couldn't expect that same quality in Ireland.

I, as well as many of you, have witnessed the perils of tenured professors who use and teach outdated software and methods that seem lost in today's complex, global world. Comfort and tradition plague academics, at least in the classroom. The transference of new methods, technologies, and means for *making things better* is vital to amplified quality in healthcare. Thus, aligning the needs in healthcare (e.g., greater patient satisfaction, reduced costs, etc.) should also align to curricula. Sure, professionals in the field need to understand the basics on which their field is intended to serve, but they also need to be able to think creatively in making healthcare a better industry. From more effective communications internally and externally without the historical egotism and lack of technical translation to instilling more than just medical procedures and jargon over the course of a decade, healthcare should be met with innovative quality improvement methods designed and implemented by those that can immediately affect change.

Critical Q&A

Do you feel that enough medical device simulation is facilitated in universities to educate students about procedures before the products go to market and these students become healthcare employees?

They are typically taught how to use medical devices, and so are good technicians. Oftentimes, however, the judgment on when to use expensive new technology is not taught, so an emerging doctor falls prey to the vendor representatives who push him to overutilize the technology. A great deal more time spent on judgment and decision making and much less spent on simply becoming a technician.

—James Rickert

What is the greatest challenge of using automation in medicine?

There are too many medical errors. The concept of eliminating all the human steps is a sound and thorough idea from an industrial engineering perspective. The reason that computerized order entry systems fail is that they don't take into account that what you've done to improve the amount of hand motions and work effort by a doctor is in reality more work on his part. A lot of doctors will tell you that you've transferred the amount of work from someone else to him. Now, he works 70 hours a week and you've upset his equilibrium because he's doing things that he is not getting paid for. That's one of the major push-backs to using automation—it saves something in one area but puts a burden on someone else. You have to figure out how to turn the automation into a win-win technique that is properly managed.

—Dean Athanassiades

What is the most ignored conversation in the healthcare debate?

Probably the most ignored conversation in the healthcare debate is articulating the purpose of the publicly funded healthcare system. Is it intended to be a "safety net" for catastrophic health events, or is it the ultimate "life, liberty, and pursuit of happiness health intervention model" intended to medically solve or resolve all of our poor health choices (smoking, drinking, drugs, and other high-risk behaviors)? Where do elective surgeries and those myriad "convenience" procedures fit in, and who should pay for them?

—Junell Scheeres

You've spoken on water applications and nanomedicine as the two areas that will benefit most from nanotechnology. Why?

Water is going to be important. A lot of people are researching filter systems using carbon nanotubes, nanoparticles, and other things. There are philanthropic organizations that are committed to do things like cleaning drinking water everywhere, such as the Bill and Melinda Gates Foundation. The alternative is usually colonic diseases and millions of kids die because of bad water. In medicine, most people opt for exotic devices or drugs because of fear of death (it's the best motivator in the world). Fear of death compensates for a lot of reservations people have about health and safety.

—David Berube

Chapter 8

Health Is the Law

At the start of 2009, the White House released a series of documents on healthcare reform. Barely weeks into the Oval Office, President Barack Obama was charged with making good on his numerous campaign speeches on coverage for most Americans and eventual coverage for all.

The Office of Management and Budget outlined the goals that an allocated budget of $630 billion over the next 10 years, not including Secretary of Health and Human Services Kathleen Sebelius's soliciting of additional funding in 2013 to support training and communication, would help achieve in the way of financing reforms to our healthcare system. A short summary of these goals cannot even begin to hold weight against the "document" that has become our nation's go-to guide for what our healthcare reform actually is. Measuring how the bill adds up to the eight principles the president promised will be attached to every dollar spent on the transformation is likely impossible, but they are worth defining.

The president said that he would adhere to the following set of principles in the process of reforming healthcare:

- Guarantee choice of health plans and physicians in which people will be allowed to keep their own doctor and their employer-based health plan.

- Make health coverage affordable through reducing waste and fraud, high administrative costs, unnecessary tests and services, and other inefficiencies that drive up costs with no added health benefits.
- Protect families' financial health by reducing the growing premiums and other costs American citizens and businesses pay for healthcare. Protecting people from bankruptcy due to catastrophic illness falls into this category.
- Invest in prevention and wellness through public health measures proven to reduce cost drivers in our system— such as obesity, sedentary lifestyles, and smoking—as well as guarantee access to proven preventative treatments.
- Provide portability of coverage, meaning that people should not be locked into their job just to secure health coverage, and no American should be denied coverage because of preexisting conditions.
- Aim for universality, meaning the plan must put the United States on a clear path to cover all Americans.
- Improve patient safety and quality care, ensuring the implementation of proven patient safety measures and providing incentives for changes in the delivery system to reduce unnecessary variability in patient care. The plan must also support the widespread use of health information technology with rigorous privacy protections and the development of data on the effectiveness of medical interventions to improve the quality of care delivered.
- Maintain long-term fiscal sustainability in which the plan must pay for itself by reducing the level of cost growth, improving productivity, and dedicating additional sources of revenue.

Bent says that most lawsuits in the medical field relate to vaccines and diagnostics, but that will change with the new laws.

Because this is a heavily regulated industry, there are always sweeping issues with such expensive government oversight. Something can hurt someone. On the drug side, the FDA authorized commercialization of drugs, quality control of modern manufacturing, and distribution chain. There are functions by the state. Nevertheless, you see a lot of drug products that end up being in litigation. Conversation goes into the statute that gives FDA jurisdiction. Preemption says that state litigation of allegations of injury due to a design flaw cannot be heard at the state level, only the federal level, and there are limits on recovery. With mass-produced and mass-marketed products, people get hurt, people die—it's almost like a firearm. With something that has life and death results, someone has to bear the cost to society, whether it is the consumer, the government, insurance, the manufacturer. This is a constant battle.

New pressures for governmental action and a confused, disenchanted public collided at the start of conversations around the first real chance of passing healthcare reform since President Obama's several past predecessors called for it.

Passions ran high, and Zarr was one of countless physicians arm in arm at many of the well-attended forums. Several members of Physicians for a National Health Program (PNHP) were even arrested for disrupting a congressional hearing on healthcare reform. Zarr recalls:

PNHP offered to be on congressional panels and we were turned down. Many physicians feel that the last available route in being heard is civil disobedience. I have an eight-month-old at home. I have spoken to my wife about participating in the demonstrations. But it is my firm belief that this is not a democracy if we can't get a seat at the table. It's no secret that members of Congress have taken thousands, even millions, of dollars from insurance companies and pharma to fund their campaigns. Insurance companies are a business.

We are at the end of our line. There are about 16,000 members of PNHP. There are about 785,000 licensed medical practitioners in this country, and the majority sympathize. Every decade has left us with more people suffering and needless dying. Lack of political will is an obstacle. We have to reform political campaigning. There is already a revolution of ideas. There will ultimately be a revolution on the streets by people in white coats. There must be a public outpouring. Doctors and patients will demonstrate. We have to change the way we do health records, chronic disease management, and shaping the work force. But putting the right incentives back for practicing medicine is key. Reimburse properly for the work that is done. Give access to care, it should not be a struggle. Power, wealth, and influence of pharmaceutical and insurance companies is hard to crack. But single payer makes sense. It's just a matter of time before people take to the streets.

Six months into his presidency, President Barack Obama had already made a variety of changes to U.S. healthcare. According to the July 2009 report by the White House:

■ The president signed the Children's Health Insurance Reauthorization Act, which provides quality healthcare to 1.1 million kids—4 million who were previously uninsured.

■ The President's American Recovery Act and Reinvestment Act protects health coverage for 7 million Americans who lose their jobs through a 65 percent COBRA subsidy to make coverage affordable.

- The Recovery Act also invests $19 billion in computerized medical records that will help to reduce costs and improve quality while ensuring patients' privacy.
- The Recovery Act also provides:
  - $1 billion for prevention and wellness to improve America's health and help to reduce healthcare costs
  - $1.1 billion for research to give doctors tools to make the best treatment decisions for their patients by providing objective information on the relative benefits of treatments
- $500 million for the health workforce to help train the next generation of doctors and nurses

O'Quinn commented:

> If the government wants to invest millions (or billions) in healthcare, it should first invest it in teaching hospitals and clinics how to identify waste in their processes and how to eliminate it. If the current administration has an itchy legislative trigger finger, here are some other worthy targets: For hospitals and clinics, use legislation to limit internal industry politics. Create a system that incentivizes contracted physicians, employed physicians, nurses, and healthcare administration to find common ground. Too often, a change that is perceived as good by one group is perceived as bad by the other groups, which then becomes a barrier to progress. As Charles F. Kettering famously said, "The world hates change, but it's the only thing that has brought progress."

"I don't agree with nationalization of healthcare; there needs to be healthy competition," said Gorman. "True measures linked to providers and provider outcome. It should be more of an incentive-based program. When we have difficulty having access, we start making healthcare look unattractive as a profession to younger people. We should look at an approach in which everyone can achieve healthcare insurance. Healthcare quality requires the investment in people, the right jobs, the right culture, and the investment in technology. Then we have to couple that with process and create a way to creatively destruct and progressively rebuild those areas that are not working for us—whether that's access or whatever, but each phase along the continuum needs to be looked at and either fixed or eliminated."

Clearly, O'Quinn would agree with previous sections of this book on the implementation of more improvement-esque training at the academic and hospital levels. At this point, improvement is desirable regardless of the state of health reform via the White House.

Agolli is hopeful. "Our greatest achievement is vision. We as Americans are industrious and we are dreamers. When left alone without the bureaucracy and government control, we believe and achieve greatness in medicine. Our medical technology is far superior, and I would have to say that is our greatest achievement thus far."

Critical Q&A

Is the new U.S. administration moving in the right direction to improve healthcare?

There is a tremendous amount of inefficiency and waste in the way that Medicare-Medicaid has operated. There has been a complete disconnect between the actual cost of healthcare and what people see. There is no transparency. If I go for a cholesterol drug, I pay $10—maybe one-fifth or one-tenth of what the cost would be if it were a market-driven concern, so the insurance protects me from this concern, but patients do not have direct contact with this price of prescription.

To the extent that the Obama administration can put in check how healthcare is administered would be a good thing. It's all in the regulation, not so much the laws. The devil will truly be in the details. Years from now, once the posturing by Congress is done, then it gets down to how the regulations are implemented. This will depend on administering this after Obama is out of office. I have a fear of rationing of healthcare—I've seen it in other countries. They literally ration healthcare; if a person is considered to be too old, the government will not pay for it. I grew up in a system in which that was not the case, but if we get there, it will be a sad day.

The fact that we spend 14 percent of care given in the last six months of life, that doesn't make any sense. There is no easy answer, but something has to change. Money at the end of life, it's questionable—we're taking money from prenatal care. Some of these issues aren't as acute in the medical device industry, but they just got through a sweeping bill providing recovery funds for the digitalization of medical records. All kinds of errors occur in that area. The prospect of unintended consequences is very great. That's a slice of what's ahead. The use of 21st century technology to keep track of patient data will have a huge impact.

—Steve Bent

Are there too many general hospitals and not enough specialty facilities or the reverse situation here in the States?

I think healthcare facility services and offerings could be better managed. This may be the best place government can intervene. Certificate of need should influence the licensing of healthcare facilities within a geographic area or region. Community and public hospitals are currently under incredible financial strain due to privately funded facilities drawing off high reimbursable and more profitable business lines and services (like cardiac, orthopedic, and women's services), while leaving the community hospital to fund high-cost, low-return services as well as support an indigent or uninsured population.

—Junell Scheeres

Chapter 9

Still in Development

When research dollars are entrusted in a scientific project that spans years to run its course, the money is allocated for a promise that an idea will morph into an invention that can potentially change the world and help medicine evolve. We don't hear about the pills that are never bottled, the equipment that never makes it into a surgical theater, or the ointment that never touches skin. The failed experiments are documented, and the materials either trashed or stored away for the next go-round. And some scientists are out of a job, yearning for another committee to have faith in their proposal.

Like fantasies that are never meant to be fulfilled, some ideas are grand and convincing, but they're not meant to make it into medicine. We do know that certain areas have more credibility and demand. Here, you'll find a roundup of some of healthcare's most fascinating and well-funded research initiatives. Will these inventions transform medicine? Let's take a look.

Nanomedicine: Since launching in 2005, the National Institutes of Health (NIH) Roadmap's Nanomedicine Initiative has centered on profound benchmarks targeting the year 2015. In general, nanomedicine refers to highly specific medical intervention at the molecular scale for curing disease or repairing damaged tissues, such as bone, muscle, or nerve. NIH explains that a nanometer is one-billionth of a meter, too small to be seen with a conventional lab microscope. It is at this size scale—about 100 nanometers or less—that biological molecules and structures inside living cells operate. Nanotechnology involves the creation and use of materials and devices at the level of molecules and atoms.

Among the eight Nanomedicine Development Centers established by NIH, research goals include giving doctors the capability to search out and destroy the very first cancer cells that would otherwise have caused a tumor to develop in the body; remove a broken part of a cell and replace it with a miniature biological machine; and implant pumps the size of molecules to deliver life-saving medicines precisely when and where they are needed.

As these collaborative centers are staffed with so many types of experts, ranging from biologists, physicians, mathematicians, and engineers to computer scientists, this area of nanomedicine will be one to watch!

Paper drug tests and text messaging: In poor countries such as Ethiopia, tuberculosis is rampant. A new monitoring system is underway that combines paper-based diagnostics with text messaging technology to help health organizations give patients another incentive to adhere to the drug regimen that may otherwise be abandoned after free prescriptions run out.

The Innovations in International Health program at MIT has developed a simple test that detects metabolites of the tuberculosis drug in urine. The metabolite reacts with chemicals in the paper, revealing a numerical code. The test is taken on a daily basis, with the results being transferred to a central database for review. As an incentive, those who take the drugs for 30 days straight would be rewarded with cell phone minutes.

Personal Genome Project: Taking place at Harvard University Medical School, scientists from around the world have assessed associations between human genetic variation, physiology, and disease risk. Over time, personal genomics will contribute to this research by creating a data set of personal genome sequences that can be evaluated along with the biological, population, medical, and physical data required for association statistics. This pool of combined data may make possible preliminary screening of proposed associations prior to more rigorous or focused data collection.

Personal genomics will also supply data for additional areas of scientific research by providing new information on the kinds and levels of variation that exist generally throughout and between individual genomes. It will also provide opportunities to assess nonmedical associations that may not have as high a priority as medical studies, e.g., biometric associations. The use of personal genomic information will also be of sociological interest.

Personal genomics has immediate importance to healthcare. A personal genome will provide, at a minimum, the information content of a large number of individual genetic tests. In some cases, this information will predict risk for serious disease that will encourage follow-on tests or medical interventions; in others, it will encourage long-term surveillance for signs of disease development, but a great deal of the information will be neutral or of uncertain significance.

Two high priorities for the field of personal genomics are to develop the education and support services that will enable individuals to understand and use their personal genomic information, and to raise awareness of the implications of personal genomics for doctors, medical educators, medical economists, insurers, and policy makers. Stakeholders in the field of personal genomics must actively foster collaborations that will develop approaches to addressing these implications.

What determines whether a particular treatment is effective or leads to severe side effects relates to our genes. Personalized medicine holds the promise of tailored medical treatments based on genetic information, rather than a one-size-fits-all approach.

Personal genome sequences will give their owners new information about themselves to assimilate into their lives. Information with implications for personal healthcare may lead to medical interventions or monitoring activities; other information may be sources of personal insight, curiosity, and speculation. People may find they have gene variants that are proposed or speculated to be associated with physiological and psychological traits. Individuals will find new and creative uses for personal genome information, e.g., friends may swap sequence information about genes of common interest.

A principal need will be to provide educational resources that will help individuals identify and distinguish false claims, guesses, speculations, and hypotheses with different degrees of confirming evidence. But a second need will be to develop mechanisms to encourage individual curiosity about genomics and channel it into public appreciation in and interest about new areas of scientific research.

Adoption of personal genome sequencing will create a marketplace for commercial products and services that promise to enhance the use or analysis of genomic information by individuals, healthcare professionals, and others. As such commercial products become available, it will become increasingly important to have mechanisms that review them and provide information as to whether they properly perform their advertised functions.

These reviews could potentially range from FDA approval for products associated with specific medical

applications, to industry-developed standards or product
rating conventions, to evaluations by independent critics,
academics, or watchdog organizations, and to informal
user experience reports in periodicals or on the web.

Skin spray gun: Created by the Armed Forces Institute
of Regenerative Medicine to heal wounds rapidly, the
method sprays skin stem cells onto an open wound and
utilizes an innovative wound dressing that serves as a bio-
reactor, nurturing the sprayed-on cells. Using the patient's
own cells, the gun has been attempted on 16 burn
patients at the Berlin Burn Center, achieving more success
than a typical skin graft. The new skin appeared natural,
having come from the person's actual pigment cells.

Surgical lasers and dyes: Using surgical lasers and light-
activated dyes, the scars of serious surgery could become
an unpleasant thing of the past. With the number of dyes
that are activated in the presence of light, researchers are
honing in on the transfer of electrons between the dye
molecule and collagen, the major structural component
of tissue. In a process called nanosuturing, the molecular chains of collagen bond to each other; the area of a
wound is then painted and illuminated with light before
the sides of a wound are knitted together.

At the heart of the trials is the Wellman Center for
Photomedicine at Massachusetts General Hospital, a facility already at the cutting edge of using and understanding
light to improve health and advance medical science.
The Wellman Center for Photomedicine is responsible
for a number of research discoveries, including a light-
activated treatment for age-related macular degeneration
and glaucoma, laser lithotripsy to remove impacted
kidney stones from the urinary tract, nonscarring skin
treatment for the safe removal of vascular and pigmented
birthmarks and other dermatological uses, and a treatment called fractional resurfacing for aging skin changes,
which stimulates the skin tissue by an array of millions of

microscopic laser beam spots. Skin wrinkles, laxity, and pigmentation due to chronic sun exposure are improved.

Tongue–eye system: Developed at the University of Wisconsin–Madison, a tongue-stimulating system translates images detected by a camera into a pattern of electronic pulses that trigger touch receptors. It's also been proven that the tongue is a prominent place on the body that receives visual information and transmits it to the brain. Once on-the-tongue sensations become shapes and features, the tongue virtually functions as an eye. We rely on the brain to interpret images correctly, not the eye, so blind people using this system have reported the recognition of shapes and motion.

According to the Gale Group, the Wisconsin researchers' tongue display system begins with a camera connected by cables from a control box. Another cable, which is flexible and flat, extends from the box directly to the blind person's tongue (like a lollipop). Stimulation from the cable's electrodes produces sensations that subjects describe as tingling or bubbling. For now, participants report modest shapes and shadows, and the size of the apparatus is big and blocky, but with the availability of nanotechnology, the whole application could be taken down in size to be more portable as the research evolves.

Besides the fundamental gift of sight, the tongue–eye system could be used for military purposes, such as ground soldiers being alerted of the presence of enemies and tanks.

Chapter 10

Conclusion

The U.S. healthcare system is large, dynamic, complex, and multifaceted. It consists of many participants—including doctors, patients, hospital administrators, insurers, health product companies, and regulators—who have vital roles. Although each of these groups seeks to improve patient health and well-being, they often work in unassociated or fragmented ways that compromise the quality and value of care.

The opportunities and cooperative strategies to improve the efficiency and effectiveness of care throughout the nation are endless. But do the choices make sense? Are they measurable? Are they cost-effective, or would the time it takes to experiment and assemble project teams even be worth the expense of getting to a satisfactory starting point?

"If you have problems with your feet, you need a podiatrist," said O'Quinn. "If you have a broken hip, you need an orthopedist. If you need a wound dressed, you need a nurse. Clinicians receive excellent training on how to repair our bodies. Depending on what is broken, we call the clinician with the appropriate skill set. But what if it's not a body that's broken? What if it's a process that's broken? Clinicians are not trained to repair processes. That's not to say some can't do it. Some may even be good at it. But even if a proctologist knows how to get my wisdom teeth out, I'm still calling the oral surgeon first. If a process is broken, my first call is going to be to a process expert."

A process expert alone cannot adequately address a poor clinical process. A clinician alone cannot adequately address a poor clinical process. However, combine clinicians and process experts on a team and the efficiency with which a clinical process is addressed, as well as the effectiveness of the improvement, increases dramatically. I cannot tell you how many times I—as a consultant—have heard the question in a number of industries, "Are you an expert in X industry?" I can almost sense those words coming out of their mouths before they even separate their lips. It's a common question for a consultant, and my response is simply, "I don't need to be an expert in industry X." There are folks that understand the market, understand the language, the behavioral aspects of the organization and its staff, and historical failures and successes of the industry. I need to be the improvement expert, someone who understands what is required to move an organization from stagnation or poor performance to one of high performance and capability. Couple those skills with current healthcare practitioners and your current staff—whether through the use of consultancies or by applying what you've learned in this book internally—and you're well on your way to achieving success.

Within this book, you've read the stories of experienced clinicians, consultants, executives, and numerous others on the topic of healthcare improvement as tied to an array of health-related services and work areas. In addition, these stories, facts, and opinions have been injected with various—some simple and some more complex—improvement methods and recommendations for affecting change, regardless of the health-related institution in which you're engaged.

As a consultant that has a passion for quality improvement, I implore you to take these readings to heart, and try it out for yourself within your own organization. I bet you'll find success. And if you do not, then you haven't tried hard enough.

As a citizen of the United States and one that has and will continue to require health services just as any other human being, don't just try it, but institutionalize improvement practices and innovation. The nation, and the world, will be better for it.

Lastly, as your friend, I would enjoy hearing about your experiences. Let's share these experiences together. Visit my website (http://www.causeforimprovement.com) and add yourself to the cause for improvement.

Bibliography

Chapter 1

Cross, Candi S. *20 Ways to Look and Feel Your Best*. Excerpts from interview with "Anya Hanes."

Progressive Centers of America. Available at http://progressivemedicalcenter.com/page/our-purpose/.

Schimpff, Stephen. 2007. *The Future of Medicine*. Nashville, TN: Thomas Nelson.

Chapter 2

Bohn, Kevin. 2009. Man Says He Lost Part of Finger in Fight at Health-Care Rally. CNNpolitics.com, September 4. Available at http://politicalticker.blogs.cnn.com.

Business Wire. 2005. Handling the "Meeting after the Meeting"; Top Female Hospital CEOs Offer Insights in Roundtable Sponsored by PHNS. May 10. Available at http://findarticles.com/p/articles/mi_m0EIN/is_2005_May_10/ai_n13680756/.

Hacker, Jacob S. 2009. A Road Map to Healthcare Reform. *Christian Science Monitor*, February 3.

Kanne, Aaron K., and Tom Best. SHS Roundtable with the Experts: Summarizing Healthcare Improvement Challenges. Institute of Industrial Engineers. Available at http://www.iienet2.org/PrinterFriendly.aspx?id=13696.

Mitchell, Luke. 2009. Sick in the Head. *Harper's Magazine*, February, pp. 33–44.

Moore, Ron. 2007. *Selecting the Right Manufacturing Tools*. Burlington, MA: Elsevier.

Rapoport, Philip Jacobs, and Egon Jonsson. 2009. *Cost Containment and Efficiency in National Health Systems*. New York: Wiley-Blackwell.

Chapter 3

Bloch, Sidney, and Stephen A. Green, eds. 2009. *Psychiatric Ethics*, 4th ed. New York: Oxford University Press.

Eckenfels, Edward J. 2008. *Doctors Serving People*. Piscataway, NJ: Rutgers University Press.

Lefkowitz, Bonnie. 2007. *Community Health Centers*. Piscataway, NJ: Rutgers University Press.

Snow, Mary, and Ashley Fantz. 2008. Woman Who Died on Hospital Floor Called "Beautiful Person." CNN.com, July 3. Available at http://www.cnn.com/2008/US/07/03/hospital.woman.death/.

Swanson, Doug J. 2009. State of Neglect: Texas Law Lets Hospitals Hide Problems. *Dallas Morning News*, January 11. Available at http://www.dallasnews.com/sharedcontent/dws/news/longterm/stories.

Chapter 4

Huvane, Kate. 2008. Follow That Infection. *Healthcare Informatics*, June.

Huvane, Kate. 2008. Quick Check-In. *Healthcare Informatics*, October.

Huvane Gamble, Kate. 2009. Connecting the Dots. *Healthcare Informatics*, January.

National Center for Health Statistics. 2005. New Study Shows Limited Use of Electronic Medical Records. CDC. Available at http://www.cdc.gov/nchs/pressroom/05news/medicalrecords.htm.

Chapter 5

Bookman, Milica Z., and Karla R. Bookman. 2007. *Medical Tourism in Developing Countries.* New York: Palgrave-McMillan.

Deloitte Center for Health Solutions. Medical Tourism Report.

Einhorn, Bruce. 2008. Checking into Bumrungrad Hospital. *Business Week*, March 17. Available at http://www.businessweek.com/globalbiz/content/mar2008/gb20080312_91880.htm.

Kirby, Tony. Trends in Health Tourism, Buying and Selling of Health Services and Movement of Healthcare Workers. *Medical News Today.* Available at http://www.medicalnewstoday.com/articles/136325.php.

Woodman, Josef. 2008. *Patients Beyond Borders.* Chapel Hill, NC: Healthy Travel Media.

Chapter 6

Gold, Lauren. 2009. Sick in America: Healthcare Reform Will Only Come with Public Anger, Says Doctor-Author. *Chronicle Online*, April 21. Available at http://www.news.cornell.edu/stories/April09/garsonCover.html.

Herzlinger, Regina. 2007. *Who Killed Healthcare?* New York: McGraw-Hill.

Kotlikoff, Laurence. 2007. *The Healthcare Fix.* Cambridge, MA: MIT Press.

Chapter 7

Cohn, Jonathan. 2009. This Won't Hurt a Bit. *The New Republic*, February 18, pp. 18–21.

Dallas Morning News. 2006. Swiss Health-Care System Might Serve as Model for U.S. *Pittsburgh Tribune-Review*, February 26. Available at http://www.pittsburghlive.com/x/pittsburghtrib/print_427691.html.

Chapter 8

Office of Management and Budget. FY 2010 Fact Sheet: Transforming and Modernizing America's Healthcare System. Available at www.whitehouse.gov.

Chapter 9

Gravitz, Lauren. 2009. Laser Show in the Surgical Suite. *Technology Review*, April, pp. 88–90.

Schimpff, Stephen. 2007. *The Future of Medicine*. Nashville, TN: Thomas Nelson.

Shachtman, Noah. 2010. Seeing Tongue, Spray-On Skin, Transplanted Hand: Top Officer Encounters Military's Extreme Medicine Wing. *Wired*, April 19. Available at http://www.wired.com/dangerroom/2010/04/spray-on-skin-and-seeing-tongues-top-officer-meets-militarys-extreme-medicine/.

Singer, Emily. 2009. A Hole in the Genome. *Technology Review*, April, p. 82.

Singer, Emily. 2009. TB Drug Compliance. *Technology Review*, April, p. 13.

Technology Review Custom Team. 2009. Making Medicine Personal. *Technology Review*, April, p. 12.

Interviews

Agolli, Gez, managing director and doctor of naturopathic medicine, Progressive Medical Centers of America

Athanassiades, Dean, healthcare informatics consultant

Bent, Steve, Life Sciences Division, Foley & Lardner LLP

Berube, David, professor of communications and nanostudies and technology studies, North Carolina State University

Campbell, Donald H., MD, MBA, FACS, senior vice president physician leadership, WellStar Health System

Chavanu Gorman, Kathleen, chief operating officer, Children's National Medical Center

Debusk, Charles, vice president of performance and process improvement, Universal Health Services

Levy, Nelson Luiz Ferreira, CEO, Bionext Brazil

Lynch, John, CEO, Merrion Pharmaceuticals Ireland

Noon, Chuck, professor of statistics of operations and management science, University of Tennessee

O'Quinn, Paul, senior performance improvement consultant, Carilion Clinic

Rickert, James, orthopedic surgeon, Bedford, Indiana

Scheeres, Junell, president, LS2 Performance Solutions, LLC

Simpson, Stephen, director of life sciences, Science Foundation Ireland

Woodman, Josef, CEO, Healthy Travel Media

Yih, Yuehwern, PhD, professor and director of Smart Systems and Operations Laboratory, Purdue University School of Engineering

Zarr, Robert, medical director of pediatrics, Unity Healthcare, Inc.

Index